BUILD

EVERY FOUNDATION WILL BE *TESTED.*

> 31 DAY
> DEVOTIONAL

JASON NEVILLE
with MIKE MARTIN

Copyright 2024 PCCF

All rights reserved. No part of this book may be reproduced, stored, or transmitted by any means-whether auditory, graphic, mechanical, or electronic- without written permission of both publisher and author, except in the case of brief excerpts used in critical articles and reviews. Unauthorized reproduction of any part of this work is illegal and is punishable by law.

For more information, please contact:

Jason Neville
Praise Chapel Christian Fellowship

3034 E. Gage Avenue
Huntington Park CA 90255
(562) 254-5498

www.praisechapelcf.com

Published by Praise Publications

All rights reserved printed in the United States of America.

JASON NEVILLE

FOLLOW JASON NEVILLE

- @PASTORJNEVILLE
- JASON NEVILLE
- FROS'T
- JASON FROS'T NEVILLE
- PRAISECHAPELCF
- PRAISE CHAPEL CHRISTIAN FELLOWSHIP

Contents

Acknowledgment vii
Introduction ix

Building on the Solid Foundation of Christ 1
Building on Wisdom 5
Built Solid 9
Built on the Rock 13
Clay in the Hands of the Master Potter 17
Cleansing Waters of Transformation 23
Confident in His Faithfulness 27
Dwelling with God 31
Embracing the Promise 35
Encouragement through Community 39
Faithful in the Little Things 43
Finishing the Race with Faith 49
Follow Me 53
God the Master Builder 57
God's Abundant Grace 61
God's Masterpiece 65
Grace Alone 69
Growing in Grace 73

In the Potter's Hands..77
Living Out the Word 83
More than Conquerors through Christ 87
Pressing On Toward the Goal 91
Rooted in Trust... 95
Soaring on Wings of Faith 99
The Cornerstone of Faith.. 105
The Rock of My Salvation 109
The Sure Foundation.. 113
The Unfailing Promise of God 119
The Wise Builder.. 125
Unchanging 129
We Are God's Field and Building.. 133

Acknowledgment

Thank you to my parents Mike & Donna Neville for raising me in the ways of the Lord and instilling in me biblical values which still hold true to this day. You taught me the importance of a solid foundation and to always put Jesus first. You showed me through your example what a joy it is to serve the Lord and to always "Trust in the Lord with all my heart and do not lean on my own understanding. In all my ways acknowledge Him, And He will make my paths straight. (Prov 3:5-6) I am eternally grateful for the example you have set before me.

Thank you to my sister Nichelle and brother-in-law Randy for all your continued love and support.

I would also like to thank my Grandparents, some of whom have already passed on to glory but have made a huge impact on my life. Grandpa McCamish (Daddy Pa as I call him), Nancy, Grandma Behealer, Grandpa Bill, Grandma and Grandpa Neville (Nanny & Poppo as I call them) all of whom I am very grateful for.

Thank you to my entire family, relatives, and friends for all of your encouragement, prayers, and support. I love you all very much and I'm very grateful to you.

Thank you to Praise Chapel Christian Fellowship, I count it an honor to serve this body of believers. God has truly shown Himself faithful to our church and the fellowship of churches around the world, Let us continue to win, build, and send until the wheels fall off.

I want to give a big thanks to my writing partner Mike Martin, an incredibly gifted writer who has encouraged me and helped me turn the vision of my books into a reality.

Thank you to my friend Eddie Reynolds for always being a constant encouragement in my life and a true friend through thick and thin. We have traveled together laughed and cried over the last 30-plus years and are still preaching the Gospel.

I also would like to thank every church, Pastor, and ministry that has opened their doors to my ministry over the years. It is truly an honor to serve the body of Christ and for that I am humbled.

Until His Return let's keep Building.
Jason Neville

Introduction

In the year 27 AD, around the time Emperor Tiberius decided to leave Rome in order to spend the rest of his reign in isolation, an enterprising former slave by the name of Atilius launched his plan to make a fortune by profiting from the insatiable Roman appetite for entertainment. The infamous result of his scheme was notable enough to be mentioned by the historians, Tacitus (c. 56-117) and Suetonius (c. 69-122).

Atilius' plan, according to Tacitus, was to make as much money as he could by entertaining the Roman population, while at the same time minimizing his business expenses as much as possible. With this in mind, he began constructing an amphitheater in the town of Fidenae, located a short distance to the north of Rome. Atilius obtained a full docket of gladiators and pressured for the arena to be completed with utmost speed so that he could start making money.

In this greedy frame of mind, Atilius encouraged his builders to cut corners, exchanging safety for haste. For his first error, he did not lay a sturdy foundation for his amphitheater. Instead, he started building on uncertain ground. The amphitheater, itself, was built of wood—which was not uncommon—but, once again, speed of construction was emphasized over quality. Despite the questionable assembly of the haphazardly made structure, Atilius' amphitheater must have looked convincingly presentable once it was completed. After running a massive advertising campaign, his opening gladiatorial show managed to attract the attention of tens of thousands of spectators.

The Roman population must have either been ignorant of Atilius' construction methods or simply did not care, for, on the day of the grand opening, endless masses of Romans arrived at Fidenae to see the show. Thousands upon thousands of spectators shuffled into the rickety wooden amphitheater to find their splintery seats. Just as he had dreamed, Atilius achieved a full house on his opening day, packing men, women, and children into his cheaply made venue. There is no telling how long the show lasted. Hopefully, the unsuspecting onlookers received some enjoyment before tragedy brought the gladiatorial games crashing to an end.

Although Atilius' amphitheater had enough enticing aesthetics to lure tens of thousands of people inside, it was not adequately built to handle the weight of so many people. Eventually, the creaking of the wood gave way to loud cracks, and the cheering of the crowds turned into screams. While the structure was fully packed, the amphitheater suffered a total collapse, crushing and trapping thousands of people in the rubble. Many of those who did not die instantly during the collapse, later succumbed to their injuries during the days it took to excavate the survivors from the debris. The casualties resulting from the incident were enormous—Suetonius claimed 20,000 people died in the collapse, but Tacitus raised the number to 50,000. Ironically, Atilius was not among the injured.

According to Tacitus, the incident inspired an outpouring of goodwill from the leading Roman citizens. The wealthy were said to have opened up their villas to provide shelter to the injured. Medical aid, as well as food and drink, was also donated in great abundance to those affected by the catastrophe. The Roman Senate, too, did its part in the aftermath of the tragedy. They hunted down Atilius and sentenced him to exile. Finally, to prevent future deaths, the Senate also imposed heavy regulations on the entertainment industry.

In Matthew 7 Jesus talked about two types of houses. In all probability, there was no difference in the materials, appearance, or size of these two houses for most houses in Jesus' day were built the same and looked the same. The difference in these two houses had to do with the foundation.

When Jesus talked about building houses, He was referring to building lives.

Take a look at the parable in Matthew 7:24-27; "Therefore everyone who hears these words of mine and puts them into practiceis like a wise man who built his house on the rock.The rain came down, the streams rose, and the winds blew and beat against that house; yet it did not fall, because it had its foundation on the rock.But everyone who hears these words of mine and does not put them into practice is like a foolish man who built his house on sand.The rain came down, the streams rose, and the winds blew and beat against that house, and it fell with a great crash."

As Christ followers, we want to be sure that we are building our lives on the solid rock of Jesus Christ. When we do, although storms will hit our lives, we will stand strong. Reading Build, the 31-day devotional, will give you the insight to do just this.

Jason Neville

CHAPTER 1

Building on the Solid Foundation of Christ

> *"For no one can lay any foundation other than the one already laid, which is Jesus Christ."*
>
> 1 CORINTHIANS 3:11 (NIV)

The Bible is inspired by God and is full of wisdom, guidance, and inspiration for our lives. One verse that holds significance in our journey of faith is 1 Corinthians 3:11. In this devotion, we will dive in and explore the depth and meaning of this verse, understanding how it serves as the cornerstone of our Christian walk. This simple verse contains spiritual insight that can guide us in our daily lives and deepen our relationship with Christ.

The One and Only Foundation: The Apostle Paul wrote these words to the Corinthian church, which was struggling with division and disputes among its members. Paul emphasizes a foundational truth that remains unshakable for all believers: Jesus Christ is the only foundation for the Christian life.

Throughout the Bible, there are many metaphors used for Jesus. He is the Good Shepherd, the Light of the World, the Bread of Life, and the Vine. In 1 Corinthians 3:11, He is the Foundation. This metaphor teaches us that without a solid foundation, a building will crumble, and so it is with our lives.

The world offers many distractions, alternatives, and counterfeit foundations to build our lives on. Some people build their lives on material wealth, while others seek fulfillment in relationships, career success, or personal achievements. However, Paul's words remind us that none of these can serve as a firm foundation for our lives.

The Unchanging Foundation: A foundation is not something that changes over time; it remains constant. In a world marked by shifting values, trends, and circumstances, the unchanging nature of Jesus Christ as our foundation is a source of great comfort.

In Hebrews 13:8, we are reminded, "Jesus Christ is the same yesterday, today, and forever." The world may change, and our circumstances may shift, but the foundation of our faith, Jesus, our Lord and Savior, remains unchangeable. We can place our trust in Him without fear of being let down.

When we build our lives on Christ, we have an unchanging foundation that is strong and secure. Regardless of the trials we face, we can stand firm, knowing that our foundation is unshakable.

The Foundation of Salvation: The foundation of Christ is not only unchanging but also the basis of our salvation. Jesus is the source of our salvation. In Acts 4:12, we read, "Salvation is found in no one else, for there is no other name under heaven given to mankind by which we must be saved." There is no alternative foundation that can offer the gift of eternal life.

Our salvation, secured by the sacrificial death and resurrection of Jesus, is the most valuable and unshakable aspect of our Christian faith. Without Christ as our foundation, there is no hope of redemption, forgiveness of sins, or eternal life.

As believers, we must recognize that the foundation of our salvation is not something we can construct or earn ourselves. It's a gift from God, made available through Christ. Our part is to accept this gift, repent of our sins, and surrender our lives to Him.

The Building Process: In 1 Corinthians 3:10–15, Paul continues to use the metaphor of a building to illustrate the importance of building our lives on the foundation of Christ. He explains that the quality of the materials we use to build on this foundation will be tested by fire. If our work endures, we will receive a reward.

This passage highlights the importance of how we live our lives as Christ followers. Our actions and choices are the building blocks that we place upon the foundation of Christ. Are we building with materials that will endure the testing fire, or are we using perishable and temporary materials?

As followers of Christ, we are called to build our lives with love, faith, obedience, and good works. These are the materials that will stand the test of time and eternity. When our lives are rooted in Christ, our actions will reflect His love and character. When we build with the right materials, our lives become a testimony to the transforming power of Christ.

1 Corinthians 3:11 serves as a powerful reminder of the foundation on which our faith is built. It's a foundation that is unchanging and enduring. When we anchor our lives in Christ, we find the strength to face the challenges of this world, knowing that our salvation is secure, and our actions have eternal significance.

As we live our daily lives, let's continually reflect on the foundation of our faith. Are we building with materials that will endure, or are we distracted by the temporary and fleeting concerns of this world? May we, as followers of Christ, strive to build our lives upon the unshakable foundation of Jesus, and in doing so, bring glory to His name and spread the message of His love and salvation to all.

CHAPTER 2

Building on Wisdom

> *"The prudent see danger and take refuge, but the simple keep going and pay the penalty."*
>
> PROVERBS 27:12 (NIV)

This verse is a powerful reminder of the importance of wisdom and discernment in our lives. In a world filled with challenges, choices, and constant change, the wisdom found in this proverb serves as a guiding light for those of us who seek to build a foundation on God's truth.

The opening phrase, "The prudent (wise) see danger and take refuge," immediately draws our attention to the quality of prudence. Prudence goes beyond mere caution; it involves foresight, careful consideration, and the ability to make wise decisions in the face of potential harm. In the context of this verse, it encourages believers to be vigilant and discerning in recognizing the dangers that surround them.

Life is filled with both visible and invisible threats. Some dangers are apparent, presenting themselves in the form of challenges, trials, or temptations. Others might be subtle and hidden by their daily routine. The prudent, however, possess a spiritual perception that allows them to see beyond the surface and discern the potential risks that lie ahead.

As followers of Christ, we are called to be wise in our walk. This requires a deep reliance on God's guidance and an unwavering commitment to seeking His wisdom through prayer, meditation on His Word, and communion with the Holy Spirit. The diligent study of Scripture equips us with the knowledge needed to identify potential pitfalls and make choices aligned with God's will.

The second part of the verse emphasizes the contrasting behavior of the simple: "But the simple keep going and pay the penalty." The term "simple" does not refer to those lacking intelligence but rather to those who lack wisdom, understanding, and the ability to foresee the consequences of their actions. The simple are characterized by a carefree or reckless attitude, ignoring the warning signs, and proceeding without thoughtful consideration.

In our spiritual journey, being simple-minded can lead to disastrous outcomes. Ignoring God's guidance and disregarding the principles found in His Word can result in unnecessary suffering and consequences. The simple may become entangled in sin's snares, fall victim to the enemy's schemes, and suffer the consequences of their poor decisions.

However, there is hope, even for the simple. Recognizing one's need for wisdom is the first step toward transformation. It involves humility, acknowledging our limitations, and turning to God for the guidance that only He can provide. The Bible assures us that if any of us lacks wisdom, we need only ask God, who gives generously to all without finding fault (James 1:5).

The imagery of taking refuge is a powerful metaphor for seeking God's protection and guidance in the face of danger. Just as a person seeks shelter from a storm, we are called to find our safety and security in God. This involves surrendering our will, trusting in His sovereignty, and allowing His wisdom to shape our decisions.

Building on the foundation of Proverbs 27:12 requires intentional steps in cultivating a life grounded in wisdom. Here are some practical steps to consider:

1. **Prioritize Prayer and Meditation:** Develop a daily habit of prayer. Seek God and His guidance in all areas of your life and meditate on His Word to gain insight and understanding.

2. **Surround Yourself with Wise Counsel:** Proverbs 15:22 reminds us, "Plans fail for lack of counsel, but with many advisers, they succeed." Seek the counsel of mature and godly individuals who can provide wisdom and perspective.

3. **Study and Apply God's Word:** Immerse yourself in the Scriptures. The more familiar you are with God's Word, the

better equipped you'll be to discern right from wrong and make wise choices.

4. **Cultivate a Teachable Spirit:** Be open to correction and instruction. A teachable spirit is a mark of wisdom, as it acknowledges the ongoing need for growth and refinement.

5. **Rely on the Holy Spirit.** The Holy Spirit is our guide and counselor. Allow Him to lead you, prompt you, and empower you to walk in wisdom each day.

Always remember that Proverbs 27:12 is a significant reminder of the critical role wisdom plays in our lives. It urges us to be vigilant, discerning, and intentional in our pursuit of God's guidance. As we build our lives on the foundation of His wisdom, we find refuge and security, avoiding the pitfalls that the simple encounter. May we, as Christ followers, continually seek the Lord's wisdom and live with wisdom in a world filled with both seen and unseen dangers.

CHAPTER 3

Built Solid

> *"Built on the foundation of the apostles and prophets, with Christ Jesus himself as the chief cornerstone."*
>
> EPHESIANS 2:20 (NIV)

Introduction: Ephesians 2:20 serves as a reminder of the cornerstone upon which our spiritual life stands: "built on the foundation of the apostles and prophets, with Christ Jesus himself as the chief cornerstone." Let's take a journey, and dive into this Scripture, to understand its relevance in our lives today.

The Foundation of the Apostles and Prophets: At the heart of Ephesians 2:20 lies a powerful metaphor—the imagery of a foundation. Foundations are not afterthoughts; they are carefully laid, providing stability and support for the structure above. The foundation of our faith, according to this verse, is composed of the foundation of the apostles and prophets, with Christ Jesus himself as the chief cornerstone.

The apostles, chosen and commissioned by Christ Himself, played an important role in establishing the early Christian Church. Their witness, teachings, and sacrificial commitment form the foundation upon which subsequent generations would build. They were eyewitnesses to the life, death, and resurrection of Jesus Christ, and their testimony forms an unshakable foundation for our faith.

In addition to the apostles, the prophets of old also contributed to this foundation. The Old Testament foretold the coming Messiah and provided insights into God's redemptive plan. Through their messages, God spoke, laying the groundwork for the revelation that would culminate in the person of Jesus Christ.

Christ Jesus Himself as the Chief Cornerstone: While the apostles and prophets form the foundation, Ephesians 2:20 emphasizes that Christ Jesus is the chief cornerstone. In ancient buildings, the cornerstone was not only foundational but also served as a reference point for the alignment and integrity of the entire structure. Likewise, Jesus Christ is the cornerstone of our faith, providing alignment to God's redemptive plan.

As the cornerstone, Jesus displays stability and reliability. He is the unchanging and eternal foundation upon which our faith rests. Christ remains steadfast, unwavering, and immovable in a world filled with uncertainties and shifting sands. Our trust in Him ensures that we are grounded in something far more enduring than the transient circumstances of life.

Reflections on the Metaphor: The metaphor of a building, with Christ as the cornerstone and the apostles and prophets as the foundation, encourages us to consider the integrity of our spiritual structure. Are we building upon this foundation, allowing Christ to be the reference point for our lives? Are the teachings of the apostles and prophets shaping the way we live out our faith?

The process of construction implies intentionality and effort. We are not passive recipients of a predetermined structure but active participants in the building of our spiritual building. Each decision, each action, and each thought contribute to the ongoing construction of our lives upon this foundation. It requires diligence to ensure that our lives align with the truths laid out by the apostles and prophets.

Practical Implications for Today: Ephesians 2:20 is not a mere historical document; it speaks to our present reality. As we navigate the complexities of the world we live in, this verse encourages us to consider the importance of the apostles' and prophets' teachings in our lives. The unchanging truths they proclaimed centuries ago continue to light our path and guide our steps today.

In a culture that often values relativism and individualism, the foundation of the apostles and prophets offers an anchor of absolute truth. Their teachings, inspired by the Holy Spirit, provide a compass that points us toward God's eternal principles. In a society where trends and ideologies may shift like the sand, the solid foundation of biblical truth remains unyielding.

The acknowledgment of Christ as the chief cornerstone challenges us to center our lives around Him. It calls for a reevaluation of our priorities, pursuits, and perspectives. Is Christ truly the cornerstone of our existence, or have we allowed other things to take precedence?

The strength of a building lies in its alignment with its cornerstone; similarly, the strength of our lives is found in our alignment with Christ.

Conclusion: Always remember, Ephesians 2:20 extends an invitation to consider and take action. It urges us to reflect on the foundation upon which we are building our lives and challenges us to ensure that it is firmly anchored in the apostles' and prophets' teachings, with Christ as the chief cornerstone. As we navigate the complexities of our faith journey, may this verse serve as a guiding light, reminding us of the unchanging truths that shape our identity and purpose in Christ.

CHAPTER 4

Built on the Rock

> *"Unless the Lord builds the house, the builders labor in vain. Unless the Lord watches over the city, the guards stand watch in vain."*
>
> — Psalm 127:1 (NIV)

In this verse, we see important truth, wisdom, and guidance for our lives. It's a verse that reminds us of the importance of acknowledging God's sovereignty in all that we do. Let's dive into this verse and explore the lessons in it.

"Unless the Lord builds the house, the builders labor in vain." This Scripture serves as a significant truth that we must grasp. It underscores the reality that without God as the foundation of our lives, all our work is in vain. As human beings, we have a natural tendency to be self-reliant, thinking that we can achieve anything through our strength and wisdom. We may build great houses, establish successful careers, and create worldly empires, but if we neglect to build our lives on the solid foundation of God's guidance and presence, all our work is meaningless.

Building a life without the Lord's involvement is living a life without Him at the center. We may accomplish many things, but if we are not aligned with God's will and purpose, our achievements will lack eternal significance. The house that God builds is built with spiritual values such as love, humility, faith, and service. These are the building blocks that make a home truly blessed, not just in material wealth but in the happiness and joy that come from living a life devoted to God.

The Bible tells us that the foundation of the house is Jesus Christ, as described in Matthew 7:24–25: "Therefore everyone who hears these words of mine and puts them into practice is like a wise man who built his house on the rock. The rain came down, the streams rose, and the winds blew and beat against that house; yet it did not fall because it had its foundation on the rock." When we allow the Lord to build our house, our lives are firmly rooted in Christ, and we become resilient in the face of life's challenges.

"Unless the Lord watches over the city, the guards stand watch in vain." This part of the verse reminds us that human efforts alone are insufficient for security and protection. While we may take every precaution to safeguard our homes and communities, it's only through God's watchful eye that true safety is assured. Human endeavors, no matter how well-intentioned, can never replace the ultimate protection that comes from divine providence.

This concept goes beyond physical safety. Just as a city needs the Lord's protection, we need His watchful care in our lives too. We are often bombarded by worries, anxieties, and uncertainties. We may try to protect ourselves through our means, but we are limited in what we can do. Only when we surrender our concerns to the Lord and trust in His guidance can we experience true peace and security.

Trusting in God's watchful care also means recognizing that He is in control, even when we cannot see the bigger picture. We live in a world filled with uncertainties, and the future can be fearful. However, when we understand that the Lord watches over us, we can rest in His sovereignty, knowing that He has a perfect plan for our lives. As the apostle Paul reminds us in Romans 8:28 (NIV), "And we know that in all things God works for the good of those who love him, who have been called according to his purpose." This assurance allows us to face each day with confidence, even when circumstances seem unfavorable.

Psalm 127:1 challenges us to shift our perspective from self-reliance to God-reliance. It calls us to reevaluate our priorities and recognize that all our efforts should begin with seeking God's guidance and continue with trusting in His protection. We must acknowledge our need for God's wisdom and strength, in every area of our lives, whether it be in our homes, our workplaces, or our communities.

As we meditate on this verse, we are also reminded of the importance of prayer. Prayer is how we invite the Lord to build our houses and watch over our cities. Through prayer, we seek God's guidance, ask for His protection, and surrender our concerns and anxieties into His hands. It's through prayer that we maintain a close and intimate relationship with our Heavenly Father, who delights in hearing and answering our petitions.

Always remember Psalm 127:1 serves as a reminder of the importance of trusting in God's sovereignty. It challenges us to reevaluate our approach to life and calls us to shift our focus from self-reliance to God-reliance. When we allow the Lord to build our houses and watch over our cities, we discover a life of purpose, peace, and security. This verse encourages us to begin each day with a prayerful heart, seeking God's guidance and protection in all that we do. By doing so, we can rest in the knowledge that our labor is not in vain and that our lives are built on the unshakable foundation of God's love and providence. May this verse inspire you to trust in God's sovereignty and experience the abundant life that comes from living in alignment with His will.

CHAPTER 5

Clay in the Hands of the Master Potter

> *"Yet you, LORD, are our Father. We are the clay, and you are the potter. We are all the work of your hand."*
>
> ISAIAH 64:8 (NIV)

In life, there are moments of significant revelation when scripture reminds us of our Heavenly Father's divine design. Isaiah 64:8 is one verse that has the power to stir the soul, offering a picture of God's intimate relationship with His children. In this verse, we are given a glimpse into the nature of our relationship with the Almighty: He is our Father, and we are the clay in the skilled hands of the Master Potter.

This verse reminds us of the truth that we are God's creation, crafted by His loving hands. Let's dig deeper into the richness of this verse to understand the significance of God as our Father and us as His clay.

God as Our Father: The relationship between God and humanity is often described in family terms throughout the Bible. Here, the prophet Isaiah addresses the Lord as "Father." This metaphor speaks to the intimacy and care that God has for His children. Just as an earthly father provides for, protects, and loves his children, our Heavenly Father does the same for us, His spiritual children. This portrayal of God as our Father emphasizes His love and concern for every aspect of our lives.

As our Father, God is not distant, who watches us from afar. He is intimately involved in our daily lives, guiding, protecting, and nurturing us. He knows our needs, our joys, our sorrows, and our dreams. This relationship with our Heavenly Father is one of profound trust and dependence. Just as a child relies on their earthly father for guidance and provision, we must trust in God's wisdom and care in our journey of faith.

We Are the Clay: Isaiah's metaphor continues with the image of humanity as clay. Clay is a substance that is moldable and pliable, easily shaped by the potter's hands. In the same way, we are entirely in the hands of our Heavenly Father. We are not self-sufficient or independent; we are dependent on God for our existence and purpose. This picture of clay reminds us of our human frailty, humility, and need for His divine, loving touch.

Just as clay must yield to the potter's design, we must yield to God's will and purpose for our lives. This submission to God's plan is an act of faith, acknowledging that His design is always better than our own. When we resist, like hardened clay, we hinder the work of the Master Potter. But when we yield and allow Him to shape us, we become vessels of beauty and purpose, ready to fulfill our divine destiny.

The Work of God's Hand: This verse highlights that we are "the work of God's hand." This phrase underscores the idea that we are not accidents or random occurrences but rather deliberate creations by the loving hand of our God. Each one of us is a masterpiece, uniquely fashioned with a specific purpose in mind.

Recognizing that we are God's handiwork is a humbling realization. It calls us to reflect on our value and worth, not because of our achievements or possessions, but simply because of who created us. We are valuable not for what we do but for who we are in God's eyes.

This truth has important implications for our self-worth and how we view others. We are called to recognize His divine fingerprints on our lives and, in turn, see them in the lives of others. This understanding leads to a deep sense of respect for the dignity of every human being.

As we consider this verse, we find both comfort and challenge. The comfort lies in the assurance that our Heavenly Father is intimately involved in our lives, shaping and guiding us with a love that knows no bounds. The challenge is to surrender to His loving design and trust in His wisdom, even when His ways seem mysterious and beyond our understanding.

Application in Our Lives: Isaiah 64:8 provides a framework for us to live in our journey as a Christ follower. It encourages us to embrace the role of clay, acknowledging our dependency on God's wisdom and guidance. Here are a few practical applications of this verse in our lives:

1. **Surrender and Trust**: As clay in the Potter's hands, we are called to surrender ourselves to God's will and trust in His perfect plan. This surrender means letting go of our ambitions, control, and self-reliance and, instead, relying on His divine wis.dom and love.

2. **Humility**: The image of clay reminds us to maintain a posture of humility in our walk with God. We must recognize our limitations and our need for His shaping and molding. A humble heart is receptive to His guidance.

3. **Dignity and Value**: Understanding that we are the work of God's hand elevates our sense of self-worth and the worth of others. Every person we encounter is a masterpiece in progress, created by the same Master Potter.

4. **Resilience**: Just as clay can be reshaped and refined, we can find hope in the fact that God can work in our lives, even during our failures and shortcomings. His hands are always ready to restore and reshape us.

Always remember that Isaiah 64:8 is a beautiful reminder of the depth of God's love and the significance of our relationship with Him. As children of God, we are not aimlessly drifting through life but are part of a divine masterpiece in the making. We can find comfort in our Heavenly Father's love and wisdom, and we can rest in the assurance that His plans for us are perfect. May this verse inspire us to yield ourselves to the Master Potter's skillful hands, allowing Him to mold us into vessels of beauty and purpose for His glory.

CHAPTER 6

Cleansing Waters of Transformation

> *"Then I will sprinkle clean water on you, and you shall be clean; I will cleanse you from all your filthiness and from all your idols. I will give you a new heart and put a new spirit within you; I will take the heart of stone out of your flesh and give you a heart of flesh. I will put My Spirit within you and cause you to walk in My statutes, and you will keep My judgments and do them."*
>
> EZEKIEL 36:25–27 (NKJV)

Everyone wants the results of what transformation looks like. It's like taking an old beat-up fifty-five Chevy and wanting it to magically become restored, without any work or sacrifice. However, commitment, work, and resources are required. The same is true of our lives. We want transformation and we want it now. But the plan of God always includes a time of cleansing and a change of heart. That's what this passage of Scripture is all about. Let's dive in and see.

Introduction: In the Book of Ezekiel, we find a promise revealing the transforming power of God. Ezekiel 36:25–27 is a passage that deals with the truth of God's redemptive love and the spiritual cleansing it offers to His people. Let's jump into this scripture, explore its depths, and draw some inspiration for our journey of faith.

The Cleansing Waters: The beginning of the verse paints a vivid image of God's cleansing work in our lives. "Then I will sprinkle clean water on you, and you shall be clean." Water holds symbolism throughout the Bible, signifying purification, renewal, and spiritual rebirth. In this context, the water represents the cleansing power of God's grace, which can wash away the stains of sin that mark our lives.

The promise is not simply an external cleansing but a deep, internal purification. God, as the Divine Cleanser, takes it upon Himself to remove the filthiness and idols that have tainted our hearts. His love is transforming, reaching into our souls to purify and renew.

A New Heart and Spirit: The next verses declare a radical transformation that transcends the external realm. "I will give you a new heart and put a new spirit within you." This promise echoes the theme of regeneration found throughout the Bible. God's desire is not just to clean the surface but to cleanse the core of our being.

The mention of a "new heart" means a complete overhaul of our innermost desires, affections, and motivations. Our old, stony hearts, resistant to the promptings of God, will be replaced with hearts that are pliable, responsive, and attuned to His will. It's a promise of a profound internal transformation that only God can accomplish.

The heart, in biblical terms, represents the center of one's being—the seat of emotions, thoughts, and intentions. The promise of a new heart signifies a radical change in our very nature, aligning our desires with God's heart.

At the same time, God promises to "put a new spirit within you." This speaks to the renewal of our spirit. The spirit experiences a rebirth under the influence of God's transforming grace. This is not a mere modification but a complete renewal, a spiritual regeneration that empowers us to live in harmony with God's divine purpose.

The Removal of the Heart of Stone: The passage goes on to say, "I will take the heart of stone out of your flesh and give you a heart of flesh." The imagery here is powerful. The "heart of stone" symbolizes a spiritual condition characterized by hardness, rebellion, and insensitivity to God's leading.

God, in His mercy, replaces our unyielding heart and replaces it with a heart of flesh. A heart of flesh is soft, responsive, and pliable—a heart capable of feeling, loving, and responding to the touch of God's grace. This transformation is a testimony of God's ability to reshape the very fabric of our being, turning stubbornness into surrender and resistance into receptivity.

The Indwelling of the Holy Spirit: The promise in this passage is the indwelling of the Holy Spirit: God says, "I will put My Spirit within you and cause you to walk in My statutes, and you will keep My judgments and do them." The Holy Spirit, the third person of the Trinity, is not merely a passive observer but an active participant, who empowers us in our spiritual journey.

God promises not only a change in our hearts but an ongoing empowerment through His Spirit. The Holy Spirit becomes the driving force behind our obedience to God's commands. It's through the Spirit's guidance and influences that we are empowered to walk in the will of God.

The phrase "cause you to walk" is a divine empowerment that transcends our human capabilities. It's God's Spirit working within us, aligning our will with His, and empowering us to live a life that reflects His righteousness. This promise declares the importance of relying on the Holy Spirit in our journey of faith.

Conclusion: Ezekiel 36:25–27 paints a portrait of God's redemptive love, revealing His commitment to purify, renew, and empower His people.

As we reflect on this passage, let's invite the cleansing waters of God's grace to wash over us, removing the stains of sin. Let's open our hearts to the transforming work of the Holy Spirit, allowing Him to replace our hearts of stone with hearts of flesh. And may we embrace the promise of a new spirit, aligning our desires with God's will.

In the light of Ezekiel 36:25–27, let's approach each day with the assurance that God's transforming power is at work within us. Through His Spirit, we can walk victoriously in life. And remember, the ever-present, ever-transforming grace of our Heavenly Father is with us on this journey, so it is not one we take alone.

CHAPTER 7

Confident in His Faithfulness

> *"Being confident of this, that he who began a good work in you will carry it on to completion until the day of Christ Jesus."*
>
> PHILIPPIANS 1:6 (NIV)

In life, we often find ourselves entangled in uncertainty. The journey of faith is no exception, marked by twists and turns, peaks and valleys. In these moments of doubt and questioning, we are encouraged to turn our eyes towards the reassuring words of Philippians 1:6. This verse serves as an anchor for our hearts, reminding us of an important truth—that the One who began the work within us is faithful to bring it to completion.

The opening words, "Being confident of this," invite us into a stance of assurance. Confidence in the spiritual realm is not rooted in our strength or abilities but is an outgrowth of our trust in the character of God. We are called to be confident not in ourselves but in the One who is both the Author and Finisher of our faith (Hebrews 12:2). This confidence is not a fleeting emotion but a steady, unwavering trust in the reliability of God's promises.

The verse continues, "That he who began a good work in you." The "good work" mentioned here is the ongoing process of sanctification—the molding and shaping of our character to reflect the image of Christ. This work was initiated by God Himself. It's crucial to understand that our journey of faith is not a self-imposed undertaking but rather a divine masterpiece created by the hands of our Heavenly Father. In our moments of inadequacy, we can take comfort in the fact that the One who spoke the universe into existence has taken a personal interest in our lives.

The language of "began" implies a starting point, a moment when God, in His infinite wisdom, set His plan for our transformation into motion. Reflecting on this truth draws our attention to the grace that precedes and undergirds our faith. It was not our merit that initiated this divine work, but God's sovereign grace. This understanding humbles us and directs our focus to the grace that sustains us.

As we live our lives, we encounter challenges that test the resilience of our faith. Yet, the verse assures us that the One who began this transforming work will complete it. The responsibility for our growth and maturity does not rest solely on our shoulders. God, in His omnipotence and love, assumes the role of the faithful gardener, cultivating the seeds of faith He has planted within us.

The phrase "will carry it on to completion" resonates with the theme of steadfastness. God does not abandon His work in the middle; He is committed to bringing it to fruition. The path of sanctification is a lifelong journey, marked by both victories and defeats. In our seasons of triumph, God rejoices with us; in our moments of failure, He extends His mercy. This completion is not based on our perfection but on God's unwavering commitment to His children.

The assurance that God will carry His work to completion offers comfort in times of uncertainty. When we encounter setbacks, wrestle with doubts, or face the complexities of life, we can rest in the knowledge that our faith is a work in progress. God, who is not bound by time or circumstance, sees the entirety of our journey, and remains faithful to His promise.

The culmination of this transforming process is designated as "the day of Christ Jesus." This points to the hope that defines the Christian faith—the anticipation of the day when Christ's redemptive work will reach its conclusion. On that day, the fullness of God's glory will be revealed, and our sanctification will find its consummation. This vision serves as a beacon light, guiding us through the challenges of the present as we fix our eyes on the ultimate destination.

Always remember, that Philippians 1:6 speaks of the essence of our Christian journey. It invites us to embrace a confident trust in the faithfulness of God, who not only initiated a transforming work within us but is committed to carrying it to completion. As we navigate the complexities of life, let's anchor our faith in the assurance that the God who began this work is both capable and faithful to bring it to completion. May this truth speak to the depths of our souls, shaping our perspective and sustaining us through every season of life.

CHAPTER 8

Dwelling with God

> *"Have the people of Israel build me a holy sanctuary so I can live among them. You must build this Tabernacle and its furnishings exactly according to the pattern I will show you."*
>
> Exodus 25:8–9 (NLT)

In the book of Exodus, we find an intimate invitation from God to His people. In Exodus 25:8–9, the Lord speaks to Moses, saying, "Have the people of Israel build me a holy sanctuary so I can live among them. You must build this Tabernacle and its furnishings exactly according to the pattern I will show you."

These verses mark a pivotal moment in the lives of the Israelites, a moment where God reveals His desire not only for a physical dwelling place but also for a deep and meaningful relationship with His people. As we dive into these verses, we'll learn truths that speak to us today, offering important insights into our journey of faith.

The first thing that captures our attention is the phrase "Build me a holy sanctuary." God, in His infinite wisdom, doesn't simply request a place of worship; He desires a holy sanctuary. This term, "holy," means separation and consecration. It signifies a space set apart for divine purposes, a place where the sacred and the average meet. As believers, we are called to be holy, set apart for God's service, and devoted to His will (1 Peter 1:16).

The call to build a holy sanctuary is a symbolic representation of God's desire to dwell within His people. It speaks of the profound truth that our bodies are now the temples of the Holy Spirit (1 Corinthians 6:19). God doesn't simply want a physical structure; He wants our hearts as His dwelling place. In the New Testament, this concept finds its fulfillment in the person of Jesus Christ, who came to dwell among us (John 1:14). Through His sacrifice, we become living temples, sanctified by His presence.

The construction of the Tabernacle and its furnishings required careful attention to detail, as God instructed Moses to build them "exactly according to the pattern I will show you." This emphasizes the importance of obedience in our worship and service to God. The details matter to God because they reflect our commitment to honoring Him with excellence. Just as the Israelites were called to build the Tabernacle according to God's specifications, we are called to live according to the pattern of Christ, aligning our lives with His teachings and example.

God's desire to dwell among His people reveals His longing for intimacy. He doesn't want to be distant, but a present and engaged God. The idea of God dwelling among us conveys His willingness to share in our joys and sorrows and to be intimately involved in the details of our lives. This truth finds its ultimate expression in the incarnation of Jesus Christ, who came to dwell among us, experiencing the fullness of human existence (Philippians 2:7).

As we reflect on these verses, we are reminded that God's desire to dwell among His people is an invitation to relationship. He is not a God who remains unattainable, but one who seeks communion with His people. This relational aspect of God's nature is woven throughout Scripture, from the Garden of Eden to the revelation of His glory on Mount Sinai. The construction of the Tabernacle becomes a tangible expression of God's desire to bridge the gap between the divine and the human and to commune with His people in a sacred space.

In our journey of faith, we are called to respond to God's invitation to intimacy. Just as the Israelites were tasked with constructing the Tabernacle, we are called to build a dwelling place for God in our hearts. This involves a commitment to spiritual disciplines, prayer, and the study of God's Word. It requires us to be intentional in creating a sacred space within ourselves where God's presence can abide.

The beauty of this invitation is that it's not exclusive to a select few. The Israelite community as a whole contributed to the construction of the Tabernacle in the Old Testament. Likewise, in the New Testament, we, the body of Christ, are called to be a dwelling place for God collectively. The apostle Paul describes the church as a "holy temple in the Lord" (Ephesians 2:21). Our unity in Christ creates a sacred space where God's presence can dwell and His glory can be revealed.

The call to build a holy sanctuary also carries implications for our worship. The Tabernacle was a place where the Israelites offered sacrifices and worshiped God. In our lives, worship goes beyond rituals; it encompasses our existence. Romans 12:1 exhorts us to present our bodies as living sacrifices, holy and pleasing to God—our spiritual worship. Our everyday actions, thoughts, and words become offerings in the holy sanctuary of our lives.

The concept of God dwelling among us challenges us to be mindful of His presence in every aspect of our lives. It calls us to cultivate a lifestyle of worship, recognizing that God is with us in our daily routines, relationships, and challenges. When we approach life with an awareness of God's presence, even the ordinary becomes extraordinary, and our average tasks become opportunities for worship.

In conclusion, Exodus 25:8–9 (NLT) invites us into an awesome journey of faith—a journey of building a holy sanctuary for God, both individually and collectively. God's desire to dwell among His people is a testament to His love, grace, and longing for intimacy. As we respond to this invitation, let's be intentional in constructing a dwelling place for God in our hearts, aligning our lives with the pattern of Christ, and offering our worship as a fragrant offering in the sacred space of our existence. May we, as the body of Christ, continue to be a holy temple where God's presence dwells and His glory is revealed to a world in need of His love and redemption.

CHAPTER 9

Embracing the Promise

> "And we know that in all things God works
> for the good of those who love him,
> who have been called according to his purpose."
>
> — ROMANS 8:28 (NIV)

Introduction: In life, we experience joy and sorrow, triumphs and trials, and we often find ourselves questioning the purpose behind the challenges we face. In those moments of uncertainty, Romans 8:28 shines as a beacon of hope, offering a promise that transcends the struggles of this world. Let's dive into this scripture and find comfort in the assurance it provides.

Understanding the Promise: "In all things" is a phrase that includes our entire lives, the highs and lows, the mountaintop experiences, and the valleys of despair. The Apostle Paul, inspired by the Holy Spirit, urges believers to anchor their faith in the unchanging truth that God is actively at work in every circumstance.

"In all things, God works for the good"—a declaration that might seem paradoxical when facing adversity. It doesn't promise a life free from challenges, but it assures us that even in the midst of tribulations, God is building a masterpiece. The good that comes is not merely a worldly definition but a spiritual reality that aligns with God's sovereign plan.

"Of those who love him"—a condition that speaks of an intimate relationship with the Heavenly Father. Our love for God is not simply an emotion but a commitment, a surrender of our will to His divine purpose. It's in this love that we find the foundation for the promise of Romans 8:28.

"Called according to his purpose"—a reminder that our lives are not accidental. God, in His infinite wisdom, has a purpose for each one of us. The circumstances we encounter, whether pleasant or painful, are woven into the fabric of His divine plan.

The Depth of the Promise: To fully grasp the depth of this promise, let's explore its implications in various aspects of our lives.

1. **Personal Struggles:** Life often presents us with challenges that seem insurmountable. Whether it's a health crisis, financial hardship, or relational turmoil, the promise of Romans 8:28 encourages us to trust that God is working in the midst of our struggles. It invites us to lean on His strength and wisdom, confident that He is using even the most difficult situations for our ultimate good.

2. **Failures and Regrets:** The burden of past mistakes and regrets can weigh heavily on our hearts. Romans 8:28 reminds us that God's redemptive power is at work, transforming our failures into stepping stones of growth. In Christ, there is forgiveness, restoration, and the promise of a new beginning.

3. **Suffering and Persecution:** The early Christians faced persecution and hardship for their faith. In the face of suffering, the promise of Romans 8:28 became a source of comfort and strength. It assured them that their suffering was not in vain and that God was working out a greater purpose, even in the midst of persecution.

4. **Unanswered Prayers:** There are times when we fervently pray for something, and it seems as though God remains silent. In these moments, Romans 8:28 teaches us to trust in God's perfect timing and wisdom. He sees the bigger picture and, in His love, answers our prayers according to His purpose, which may differ from our immediate desires.

5. **Seasons of Waiting:** Patience is a virtue that is often tested in the seasons of waiting. Whether we are waiting for a breakthrough, a change in circumstances, or a long-awaited promise to be fulfilled, Romans 8:28 encourages us to trust that God is working in the waiting. His timing is perfect, and His plan is unfolding, even when we cannot see it.

Conclusion: Romans 8:28 is an important truth that transforms the way we perceive our lives. It invites us to view our circumstances through the lens of God's providence, trusting that He is at work in every detail. This promise is a rock on which we can anchor our faith, a refuge in the storms of life.

As we navigate the complexities of life, may Romans 8:28 be engraved on our hearts, a constant reminder that our God is faithful, and His purposes are unwavering. In the tapestry of our lives, with all its joy and sorrow, let's rest in the assurance that God is weaving a masterpiece, and in the end, it will be a testament to His love, grace, and plan for our lives.

CHAPTER 10

Encouragement through Community

> "Let us think of ways to motivate one another to acts of love and good works. And let us not neglect our meeting together, as some people do, but encourage one another, especially now that the day of his return is drawing near."
>
> HEBREWS 10:24–25 (NLT)

Introduction: In this fast-paced world we live in, the value of community cannot be overstated. As Christians, we are called to live in fellowship with one another, offering support, encouragement, and love. Hebrews 10:24–25 describes this, urging believers to consider how to spur one another toward love and good deeds and to not neglect meeting together. Let's dive into the wisdom in these verses, exploring the significance of community, encouragement, and corporate worship in our journey of faith.

Verse Breakdown: This passage is a call to action, inviting believers to engage in intentional, uplifting relationships with fellow believers. Breaking it down, we find two key exhortations: the call to motivate one another to acts of love and good works, and the admonition not to neglect meeting together but to encourage one another.

Motivating One Another: The verse begins with a plea to "think of ways to motivate one another to acts of love and good works." In a world that emphasizes self-interest and individual achievement, this call to communal motivation stands out. The Christian life is not meant to be lived in isolation; rather, we are urged to consider the needs and growth of our fellow believers.

Motivation in this context goes beyond mere words; it involves intentional actions that inspire one another toward acts of love and good works. It's a challenge to actively seek opportunities to uplift those around us, fostering an environment where the love of Christ manifests in tangible, practical expressions. Whether through acts of kindness, service, or support, we are called to be catalysts for the flourishing of love and goodness within our Christian community.

Corporate Worship and Fellowship: The second part of the verse addresses the vital aspect of corporate worship and fellowship: "And let us not neglect our meeting together, as some people do, but encourage one another." The early Christian community recognized the importance of gathering regularly for worship, teaching, and mutual support. This communal aspect of faith is foundational, providing believers with a source of strength and encouragement.

Neglecting to meet together not only hinders our personal growth but also deprives the community of the unique gifts and contributions each member brings. The corporate gathering of believers is a time to worship collectively, to share in the Word, and to offer mutual encouragement. In a world that pulls us in different directions, the local church becomes a sanctuary where believers can find comfort, strength, and shared purpose.

Especially Now: The urgency of the call to encourage one another is emphasized with the words, "especially now that the day of his return is drawing near." In recognizing the imminence of Christ's return, the author highlights the critical need for a unified and supportive community of believers. The challenges of life can be overwhelming, but the anticipation of Christ's return serves as a unifying force, urging believers to stand together in faith.

Especially in times of trial, uncertainty, or cultural upheaval, the need for encouragement within the body of believers becomes even more pronounced. As the world around us grows darker, the light of Christ within us shines more brightly when we come together, supporting, and uplifting one another. The impending return of Christ serves as a powerful motivation to live out our faith authentically and to strengthen the bonds of Christian fellowship.

Application: As we reflect on Hebrews 10:24–25, let's consider practical ways to live out these exhortations in our daily lives. In our interactions with fellow believers, let's be intentional about motivating one another to acts of love and good works. This might involve acts of kindness, words of affirmation, or simply being a listening ear in times of need.

Let's prioritize regular attendance and active participation in our local church communities. The corporate worship setting provides a unique opportunity for collective growth and encouragement. As we gather to worship, study the Word, and fellowship with one another, we contribute to the strength and vibrancy of our Christian community.

In times of challenge or uncertainty, let's be mindful of the urgency to encourage one another, recognizing that the day of Christ's return is drawing near. As we stand united in faith, our collective witness becomes a testament to the transforming power of Christ in our lives.

Conclusion: Hebrews 10:24–25 is a reminder of the necessity of the Christian community. It invites us to live a life that focuses on intentional encouragement and group worship. In a world characterized by division and isolation, these verses serve as a beacon, guiding us toward a vibrant, supportive community of believers. May we heed this call, actively seeking ways to motivate one another to acts of love and good works, and may our gatherings be characterized by genuine encouragement, especially as we anticipate the imminent return of our Lord and Savior, Jesus Christ.

CHAPTER 11

Faithful in the Little Things

> *"Whoever can be trusted with very little can also be trusted with much, and whoever is dishonest with very little will also be dishonest with much."*
>
> — Luke 16:10 (NIV)

Introduction: In Luke 16:10, Jesus imparts profound wisdom on the nature of faithfulness, stating, "Whoever can be trusted with very little can also be trusted with much, and whoever is dishonest with very little will also be dishonest with much". These words challenge us to examine the depth of our faithfulness in both the seemingly insignificant and grand aspects of our lives. In this devotion, we'll explore the implications of this verse, seeking to understand the transforming power of faithfulness in the little things.

Understanding the Verse: At first glance, Luke 16:10 may appear simple. However, its implications are far-reaching and fundamental to the Christian faith. Jesus employs the principle of stewardship, emphasizing the correlation between our faithfulness to minor responsibilities and our capacity for greater ones. By doing so, He highlights the spiritual principle that underlies our relationship with God and others.

Trusted with Little, Trusted with Much: The opening phrase of the verse, "Whoever can be trusted with very little," challenges us to reconsider our perception of small tasks and responsibilities. Often, we may be tempted to downplay the significance of small actions in our daily lives. Yet Jesus calls us to recognize the divine perspective on faithfulness. Every act of faithfulness, no matter how small, has profound spiritual implications.

Consider the example of a faithful steward managing a small estate. The master observes the steward's diligence in handling modest affairs and based on this trustworthiness, entrusts the steward with more significant responsibilities. Similarly, God observes our faithfulness in the seemingly unimportant aspects of life—our attitudes, words, and actions in ordinary moments. When we prove ourselves faithful in these "little things," God deems us trustworthy for more significant assignments in His kingdom.

The Heart of Faithfulness: To dive deeper into the essence of faithfulness, we must consider the condition of our hearts. Faithfulness is not merely a checklist of tasks performed; it's a reflection of the heart's alignment with God's values. When we approach the small details of life with a heart surrendered to God, we demonstrate a willingness to obey Him in all things.

Faithfulness in the little things involves integrity, consistency, and a genuine desire to honor God. It's about living with an awareness of God's presence in every aspect of our lives, recognizing that our faithfulness in the little things ultimately testifies to our reverence for the Lord.

Dishonesty in the Little Things: Jesus warns that dishonesty in the small matters of life has far-reaching consequences. The phrase "whoever is dishonest with very little will also be dishonest with much" serves as a cautionary statement about the erosion of character. When we compromise our integrity in seemingly insignificant matters, we set a dangerous precedent for our conduct in more substantial areas of responsibility.

Dishonesty often begins subtly, with rationalizations and justifications for small compromises. Yet Jesus emphasizes the cumulative effect of such choices. A pattern of dishonesty in minor matters can lead to a pervasive lack of trustworthiness that extends to all aspects of life. The erosion of character occurs little by little, and the consequences become increasingly severe as dishonesty takes root.

The Transforming Power of Faithfulness: As we reflect on Luke 16:10, we are invited to embrace the transforming power of faithfulness. This transformation occurs not only in the external realm of our actions but, more importantly, in the inner recesses of our hearts. God desires to mold us into faithful stewards who mirror the character of Christ in every circumstance.

The journey of faithfulness begins with a conscious commitment to honor God in the little things. It involves a deliberate choice to align our values with His and to seek His guidance in the details of our lives. When we allow the Holy Spirit to shape our character, the fruit of faithfulness becomes evident in our relationships, work, and every area of influence.

Practical Application: To apply the principles of Luke 16:10 in our lives, we can engage in intentional practices that cultivate faithfulness. Here are a few practical steps:

1. **Prayerful Reflection:** Regularly reflect on your daily actions, seeking the Holy Spirit's guidance in identifying areas where you can grow in faithfulness.

2. **Study Scripture:** Immerse yourself in God's Word to understand His principles of faithfulness. Study the lives of faithful individuals in the Bible, drawing inspiration from their examples.

3. **Accountability:** Surround yourself with a community of believers who encourage and challenge you in your journey of faithfulness. Share your goals and struggles, and allow others to speak into your life.

4. **Gratitude Journaling:** Cultivate a heart of gratitude by keeping a journal of the seemingly small blessings in your life. Recognizing and appreciating God's faithfulness in the little things fosters a spirit of faithfulness in return.

Conclusion: In Luke 16:10, Jesus encourages us to embrace a life of faithfulness in both the little and the great. As we faithfully steward the seemingly insignificant aspects of our lives, we position ourselves to receive greater responsibilities in God's kingdom. The transforming power of faithfulness extends beyond our actions; it permeates the very fabric of our character, drawing us closer to the heart of God.

May we be people who live with unwavering faithfulness in the ordinary, knowing that our heavenly Father delights in those who are trustworthy in the little things. As we journey on this path of faithfulness, may our lives become a testament to the profound impact of surrendering our hearts and actions to the One who is infinitely faithful to us.

CHAPTER 12

Finishing the Race with Faith

> "I have fought the good fight; I have finished the race; I have kept the faith. Now there is in store for me the crown of righteousness, which the Lord, the righteous judge, will award to me on that day—and not only to me but also to all who have longed for his appearing."
>
> 2 TIMOTHY 4:7-8 (NIV)

Introduction: In the final chapter of his second letter to Timothy, the apostle Paul reflects on the journey of faith, using powerful imagery.

Fighting the Good Fight: Paul begins by saying that he has "fought the good fight." The Christian journey is often described as a battle, a spiritual warfare against the forces of darkness. Paul himself faced numerous trials and tribulations, both physically and spiritually, as he spread the message of Christ. This phrase implies not just any fight but a "good fight"—a fight grounded in righteousness, truth, and the love of God. It calls us to engage in the struggles of life with a perspective shaped by the values of the kingdom.

As believers, we are enlisted in a spiritual battle against sin, temptation, and the brokenness of the world. The "good fight" encourages us to stand firm in our convictions, armed with the truth of God's Word. It reminds us that our struggles are not in vain and that, with faith in Christ, we can overcome every obstacle.

Finishing the Race: "I have finished the race," declares Paul. Life is often likened to a race, a marathon demanding endurance, perseverance, and dedication. Paul uses this metaphor to emphasize the importance of continuing in the faith until the very end. The Christian journey is not a sprint but a lifelong commitment to following Christ.

Just as a runner trains, disciplines themselves, and pushes through pain to reach the finish line, so too must believers persevere in their faith. This involves consistent prayer, studying the Scriptures, and cultivating a relationship with God. The race is not about speed but endurance, not about comparison with others but about a personal commitment to the path set before us.

Paul challenges us to evaluate our spiritual journey. Have we become weary of the race? Are we running with perseverance, or have we lost sight of the finish line? The call to finish the race encourages us to endure through the trials, trusting that God's grace sustains us until the very end.

Keeping the Faith: "I have kept the faith," proclaims Paul. This statement goes beyond the mere acknowledgment of the existence of faith; it emphasizes the importance of preserving and guarding it. Keeping the faith involves unwavering trust and allegiance to God, even in the face of adversity. It means holding onto the core truths of the Gospel and living by God's Word.

In a world filled with distractions, doubts, and competing ideologies, keeping the faith becomes a huge task. Yet, Paul's words inspire us to anchor ourselves in the unchanging truth of Christ. To keep the faith is to remain steadfast in our beliefs, even when the cultural tide shifts or when personal challenges threaten to shake our foundations.

The Crown of Righteousness: As Paul reflects on his journey, he anticipates a glorious reward: "Now there is in store for me the crown of righteousness." This crown is not a symbol of worldly achievement or self-glory, but a heavenly reward bestowed by the righteous judge. It's the culmination of a life lived in devotion to Christ, marked by faithfulness, endurance, and an unwavering commitment to the Gospel.

The "crown of righteousness" is a promise for all who persevere in faith. It's not reserved for a select few but is available to "all who have longed for his appearance." This longing for Christ's return is a mark of true discipleship. It reflects a heart that yearns for the fullness of God's kingdom and eagerly awaits the day when faith becomes sight.

Conclusion: In 2 Timothy 4:7-8, Paul's words invite believers to reflect on their journey of faith. The imagery of fighting, finishing, and keeping the faith challenges us to examine our commitment to

Christ. It calls us to persevere in the face of challenges, run the race with endurance, and guard the precious gift of faith.

Always remember, as we navigate the complexities of life, let's draw inspiration from Paul's triumphant declaration. Let's fight the good fight with the armor of God, finish the race with perseverance, and keep the faith with unwavering devotion. In doing so, we, too, can anticipate the glorious crown of righteousness that awaits all who long for the appearing of our Lord and Savior, Jesus Christ.

CHAPTER 13

Follow Me

> "*Follow Me, and I will make you fishers of men*" (MEV).
>
> MATTHEW 4:19 (MEV)

In the New Testament, certain verses embrace the essence of discipleship and the transforming power of a divine call. One such profound moment is found in the Gospel of Matthew, specifically in chapter 4, verse 19, where Jesus issues a simple yet life-altering invitation: "Follow Me, and I will make you fishers of men".

1. The Call to Follow: At the heart of Matthew 4:19 lies an invitation that transcends time and culture. Jesus, walking along the shores of the Sea of Galilee, encounters two fishermen, Simon Peter and Andrew. In the midst of their daily jobs, Jesus extends a personal call, inviting them into a relationship that would redefine the course of their lives. The call to "follow Me" is not merely an invitation to join a movement; it's an invitation to intimacy, a call to walk closely with the Savior.

Jesus doesn't choose the religious elite or the esteemed scholars; instead, He selects ordinary fishermen. This choice carries a profound message: that God's call is not limited by human qualifications or social standards. It's a call extended to the humble and the broken, to those willing to respond with faith.

2. The Promise of Transformation: The second part of Matthew 4:19 unveils a promise that resonates with divine potential: "And I will make you fishers of men." This promise signifies a journey from the familiar world of fishing for literal fish to the realm of capturing hearts for the Kingdom of God.

Jesus is not merely interested in assembling followers; He is committed to transforming lives. The promise implies a divine process, a spiritual metamorphosis where individuals are molded into instruments of God's grace and vessels of His redemptive love. In accepting the call to follow, disciples become participants in the restoration, healing, and salvation of others.

3. Fishers of Men: The imagery of becoming "fishers of men" carries profound symbolism. In the context of the first-century fishing trade, the disciples were familiar with the patience, skill, and persistence required to catch fish. Jesus employs this familiar imagery to convey the essence of their new mission—to cast the net of the gospel into the sea of humanity.

Being fishers of men requires a deep understanding of the human condition and a compassionate heart that mirrors the love of Christ. The disciples, once occupied with the tangible pursuit of fish, are now commissioned to engage in a spiritual endeavor, drawing people into the transforming embrace of God's love.

4. The Contemporary Call: The call to "Follow Me" and become "fishers of men" is not confined to when Jesus walked the earth. It speaks to us today, reaching us in the midst of our own stories. Today, as we read Matthew 4:19, the same invitation extends to us—a call to follow Jesus and participate in the redemptive work of drawing others into His love.

The contemporary disciple is not exempt from the call to transformation. We are called to be fishers of men in a world that hungers for hope and reconciliation. Our nets are cast wide in the form of compassion, kindness, and the proclamation of the Good News. As we follow Christ, we become conduits of His grace, instrumental in leading others into a transforming encounter with the Savior.

5. Challenges Along the Way: While the call to follow Jesus is filled with promise and purpose, it's not devoid of challenges. The disciples faced storms on the Sea of Galilee, moments of doubt, and the weight of personal inadequacies. Similarly, we encounter obstacles and uncertainties in our journey of discipleship.

Yet, it's precisely in these challenges that the transforming power of Christ is most evident. In our weakness, His strength is magnified. As fishers of men, we navigate the turbulent waters of life with the assurance that the One who called us is faithful to equip and sustain us. The trials we face become opportunities for God's glory to be revealed through our reliance on Him.

Conclusion: Matthew 4:19 stands as a timeless invitation. It calls us to follow Jesus intimately, to experience the profound transformation He offers, and to embrace the call to be fishers of men in a world yearning for the redemptive touch of Christ.

Always remember, as we respond to this call, may we do so with hearts surrendered to the One who knows us intimately and loves us unconditionally. May we, like the disciples, set out on a journey of faith under the leadership of the One who is the Way, the Truth, and the Life. And may our lives, transformed by the power of Christ, become testimonies of His grace and beacons of hope for a world in need of the Savior's love.

CHAPTER 14

God the Master Builder

> *"For every house is built by someone, but
> God is the builder of everything."*
> — HEBREWS 3:4 (NIV)

This verse provides us with a significant and comforting reminder of God's sovereignty and creative power. In this devotion, we'll explore the significance of this verse and how it relates to other scriptures that emphasize the role of God as the ultimate builder of our lives.

Think about it. Our lives are often compared to houses or structures. Just as a house is built by someone, our lives are shaped and constructed by various factors and influences. These influences can include our upbringing, experiences, and the choices we make. We can be influenced by the people around us, the culture we live in, and the circumstances we face. However, Hebrews 3:4 reminds us that regardless of these factors, the ultimate builder of everything is God Himself.

1. **Psalm 127:1** (NIV) says, "Unless the LORD builds the house, the builders labor in vain. Unless the LORD watches over the city, the guards stand watch in vain." This verse reinforces the idea that our efforts are in vain if God is not at the center of our lives. Just as a physical house needs a skilled builder to stand strong, our lives need the divine hand of God to be built on a firm foundation.

2. **1 Corinthians 3:11** (NIV) states, "For no one can lay any foundation other than the one already laid, which is Jesus Christ." Here, the Apostle Paul reminds us that the foundation of our lives must be built on Jesus Christ. He is the cornerstone and the most crucial element of any structure. When we build our lives upon Him, we can trust that we are building on a solid and unshakable foundation.

3. **Matthew 7:24-27** (NIV) contains the parable of the wise and foolish builders. Jesus said, "Therefore, everyone who hears these words of mine and puts them into practice is like a wise man who built his house on the rock. The rain came down, the streams rose, and the winds blew and beat against that house, yet it did not fall because it had its foundation on the rock. But everyone who hears these words of mine and does not put them into practice is like a foolish man who built his house on sand. The rain came down, the streams rose, and the winds blew and beat against that house, and it fell with a great crash." This parable underscores the importance of not only hearing God's Word but also putting it into practice. When we obey God's Word and build our

lives upon His teachings, we are like the wise builder who constructs a house on a solid foundation.

4. **Isaiah 64:8** (NIV) declares, "Yet you, LORD, are our Father. We are the clay, you are the potter; we are all the work of your hand." This verse presents a beautiful picture of God as a potter, shaping and molding us as clay. It emphasizes that our lives are a product of His craftsmanship. Just as a skilled potter meticulously forms and fashions clay into a vessel of beauty and purpose, God does the same with our lives.

5. **Ephesians 2:10** (NIV) affirms, "For we are God's handiwork, created in Christ Jesus to do good works, which God prepared in advance for us to do." This verse emphasizes that we are God's handiwork, His masterpiece. He has created us with a specific purpose in mind. Our lives are not haphazardly put together, but they are intricately designed by the Creator of the universe.

Hebrews 3:4 not only reminds us of God's role as the ultimate builder but also encourages us to consider who is the builder of our lives. Are we allowing God to be the primary architect and constructor of our lives, or are we trying to build on our own? When we try to build our lives independently of God, we find ourselves laboring in vain and facing instability. However, when we acknowledge God as the builder of everything and submit to His divine plan, we can trust that our lives will be firmly established on the foundation of His love and wisdom.

As we reflect on these scriptures and the truth in Hebrews 3:4, let's remember that God is not only the builder of our lives but also the source of our strength. Just as a house requires ongoing maintenance and care, our lives need the continual guidance and presence of the Lord to flourish and stand firm in the face of life's storms.

Always remember, Hebrews 3:4, along with the supporting scriptures, reminds us of the importance of recognizing God as the ultimate builder of everything. He is the architect of our lives, the cornerstone of our foundation, and the potter shaping us into vessels for His purpose. Our role is to yield to His guidance, trust in His wisdom, and obediently follow His Word. When we do so, we can rest assured that our lives will be built on a solid foundation that can withstand the trials and challenges that come our way.

CHAPTER 15

God's Abundant Grace

> *"And God is able to make all grace abound toward you, that you, always having all sufficiency in all things, may have an abundance for every good work."*
>
> — 2 Corinthians 9:8 (NKJV)

Introduction: In this passage of scripture, we find a profound promise that speaks to the greatness of God's grace and generosity. These words written by the Apostle Paul, reveal the depth of God's love and provision for His children.

God's Abounding Grace: The opening phrase, "And God is able," sets the stage for a revelation of the capability of God that is beyond human comprehension. The creator of the universe, our God, is unrestricted. He possesses an infinite capacity to pour out grace upon His children. This grace is not ordinary; it's extraordinary, abounding in richness and completeness. It surpasses our understanding.

This abounding grace is not reserved for a select few; it's extended toward "you." The personalization of this promise speaks directly to each believer, inviting us to claim this truth as our own. God's grace is not a distant concept but a tangible reality, ready to manifest in our lives.

All-Sufficiency in All Things: The verse continues with the assurance that this abounding grace leads to "always having all sufficiency in all things." Here, the Apostle Paul emphasizes the comprehensive nature of God's provision. There is no aspect of our lives that God overlooks or neglects. In every circumstance and every need, God's grace provides more than enough.

This sufficiency is not based on our efforts or merit but is a direct result of God's unmerited favor. We can rest in the confidence that, in Christ, we lack nothing. The financial, emotional, spiritual, and relational aspects of our lives find completeness in the sufficiency of God's grace.

Abundance for Every Good Work: The verse culminates in a beautiful promise: "that you may have an abundance for every good work." God's intention goes beyond meeting our personal needs. He desires to overflow our lives with abundance so that we may be channels of His goodness to others. The abundance we receive from God is not meant to be hoarded but shared, not stored but distributed.

As recipients of God's abundant grace, we are called to be channels through which His love and kindness flow to those around us. The good works mentioned here encompass acts of compassion, generosity, and service that reflect the character of our benevolent God. Our lives, overflowing with God's abundance, become a testimony to His grace and an instrument for the advancement of His kingdom.

Implications for Our Lives: Understanding and embracing the truths in 2 Corinthians 9:8 transforms the way we perceive and live our lives as followers of Christ.

1. **Faith in God's Capability:** This verse challenges us to place our faith in the God who is able. When we encounter challenges that seem insurmountable, we can trust in His ability to provide, sustain, and overcome.

2. **Freedom from Anxiety:** The assurance of all-sufficiency in all things frees us from the burden of anxiety. As we rest in God's provision, we can relinquish our worries and anxieties, knowing that our Heavenly Father cares for us.

3. **Generosity as a Lifestyle:** The call to have an abundance for every good work prompts us to cultivate a lifestyle of generosity. By sharing our blessings with others, we mirror God's heart and participate in His redemptive work in the world.

4. **A Life of Purpose:** Recognizing that God's abundance is meant for every good work gives our lives a sense of purpose beyond personal fulfillment. We are invited to be intentional in seeking opportunities to impact the lives of others positively.

5. **Gratitude and Praise:** Thinking about God's abounding grace causes us to have a response of gratitude and praise. In acknowledging His generosity, our hearts are stirred to worship the One who provides abundantly.

In conclusion, let's be excited about the depth of God's grace as we reflect on 2 Corinthians 9:8. It's a grace that goes beyond our comprehension, meets our every need, and empowers us to live purposefully for His glory. May this verse serve as a source of inspiration, comfort for the weary soul, and inspiration for a life characterized by faith, generosity, and gratitude. In God's abounding grace, we find not only sufficiency for ourselves but an abundance for the flourishing of His kingdom on earth.

CHAPTER 16

God's Masterpiece

> *"For we are God's masterpiece, created in Christ Jesus to do good works, which God prepared in advance for us to do."*
>
> — EPHESIANS 2:10 (NIV)

This verse beautifully details the essence of our Christian journey—a journey of redemption, purpose, and divine craftsmanship.

The verse begins with a profound declaration: "For we are God's masterpiece." The term "masterpiece" carries the weight of purpose and skill. It paints a vivid picture of a master craftsman intricately fashioning a masterpiece. In this context, God is the divine craftsman, and we, His children, are His masterpieces. This truth shatters any notion of randomness or happenstance in our existence. It confirms that the creator of the universe purposefully and intricately created us.

The concept of being God's masterpiece invites us to contemplate our identity. We are not random. We are intentional creations of a loving God. The hands that formed us with purpose and love determine our value rather than societal norms, successes, or failures. In a world that often seeks to diminish individual value, Ephesians 2:10 stands as a beacon of hope, reminding us that we are cherished works of divine artistry.

The verse then unveils the purpose behind God's creative act: "created in Christ Jesus to do good works." Our existence is not a mere accident; rather, it's intricately connected to a larger purpose—to reflect the character of God through our actions. We are created in Christ Jesus, the embodiment of love, grace, and righteousness. This connection signifies that our purpose is not self-determined but rooted in a relationship with the Savior.

The phrase "to do good works" emphasizes the transforming power of our faith. As recipients of God's grace, our lives are meant to overflow with goodness and compassion. The good works are not a means to earn salvation but a natural outflow of the salvation we have received. Our actions become an expression of gratitude, a response to the unmerited love God has poured out upon us. Every act of kindness, every word of encouragement, and every display of love becomes a brushstroke in the masterpiece God is crafting through us.

The verse also states that these good works were "prepared in advance for us to do." God, in His infinite wisdom, foreknew and predestined the good works that would characterize our lives. This divine foresight challenges our understanding of time and purpose. Before we took our first breath, God had already laid out a path for us to walk in obedience and service. This realization instills awe and humility by acknowledging that our lives are part of a vast, divine story that the Creator Himself wrote.

Understanding that our purpose is preordained can be both reassuring and challenging. It reassures us that we are not living life aimlessly; rather, we are walking in the footsteps God has ordered for us. However, it also challenges us to align our will with God's and to be attentive to the promptings of the Holy Spirit. It invites us to surrender our plans and ambitions to God, trusting that His ways are higher, and His purposes are perfect.

In the busyness of life, it's easy to lose sight of our identity as God's handiwork and our calling to do good works. The demands of work, relationships, and personal aspirations can obscure the plan God is developing through our lives. Ephesians 2:10 serves as a constant reminder to pause, reflect, and realign our lives with God's purpose.

Practically, this verse challenges us to examine our daily choices, motivations, and actions. Are we intentionally living as God's masterpiece? Are we seeking opportunities to do good works, not for personal gain but as a reflection of God's love? The mundane tasks of life—whether at home, in the workplace, or in the community—become significant when infused with the understanding that they are part of the good works God has prepared for us.

As we navigate the complexities of life, Ephesians 2:10 invites us to cultivate a mindset of purpose and intentionality. It encourages us to view every interaction, every decision, and every moment as an opportunity to glorify God through our actions. Whether we find ourselves in seasons of abundance or scarcity, in times of joy or sorrow, the truth of Ephesians 2:10 remains constant—God is at work in and through us.

Always remember, Ephesians 2:10 is a powerful reminder of our identity, purpose, and the divine craftsmanship that shapes our lives. As God's masterpiece, we are not random, insignificant beings but intentional creations designed to reflect the glory of our Creator. Our purpose is woven into the fabric of our existence—created in Christ Jesus to do good works. May this truth resonate in our hearts, transforming our perspective on life and inspiring a life dedicated to the good works God has prepared in advance for us to do.

CHAPTER 17

Grace Alone

> *For it is by grace you have been saved, through faith—and this is not from yourselves, it is the gift of God— not by works, so that no one can boast.*
>
> — EPHESIANS 2:8–9 (NIV)

Introduction: Ephesians 2:8–9 unveils a profound revelation about the nature of God's grace and its role in our salvation. These verses detail the essence of Christian faith, emphasizing that our redemption is not earned through our works but is a divine gift bestowed upon us. Let's dive into the richness of Ephesians 2:8–9, exploring the depth of God's grace and understanding how it transforms our lives so that we can build our lives on it.

Saved by Grace: The opening words of Ephesians 2:8 is a significant statement: "For it is by grace you have been saved." This succinct declaration describes the central theme of Christianity: salvation is not a wage to be earned but a gift to be received. The grace mentioned here is not a mere theological concept; it is the unmerited favor of

God, an outpouring of divine love and mercy that transcends human comprehension.

The Apostle Paul, writing under the inspiration of the Holy Spirit, underscores the exclusivity of grace in the process of salvation. Our rescue from sin and the restoration of our relationship with God are not based upon our deeds or accomplishments. Instead, they hinge entirely on the generosity of God's grace. This truth strikes at the root of human pride, dismantling any notion that salvation is a reward for our efforts.

Faith as the Instrument: Having established the foundational role of grace, Paul goes on to say how this grace is appropriated: "through faith." Faith is the channel through which we receive the divine gift of salvation. It's not our work in itself, but a humble response to the grace of God. In a world that often screams for self-sufficiency and independence, the Gospel invites us to acknowledge our need for and dependence on God.

Faith involves trusting God entirely, believing in His promises, and relying on His character. It's a surrendering of our will to His divine will, an acknowledgment that salvation is beyond our human capacity. Paul's choice of words here is intentional—salvation is "through faith"—to underscore that even our ability to believe is a gift from God (Ephesians 2:8). The combination of grace and faith work together in the process of salvation.

Not of Works: To further highlight the nature of salvation, Paul reinforces the idea that our redemption is "not of yourselves; it is the gift of God" (Ephesians 2:8). The Apostle emphatically denies any claim of human boasting or self-sufficiency in the process of salvation. Salvation is not a transaction where God rewards our good deeds; it's a divine gift freely given.

This rejection of self-reliance strikes at the core of human pride. In a world that often values accomplishment and self-achievement, the Gospel stands as a counter-narrative, proclaiming that we bring nothing to the table in the realm of salvation. It's only the grace of God that rescues us from the grip of sin and reconciles us to Himself.

Verse 9 continues this theme: "Not by works so that no one can boast." Here, Paul addresses the human tendency to boast about personal achievements. The absence of boasting is not only a testament to the exclusive role of grace in salvation but also a safeguard against the corrosive influence of pride. In the economy of grace, boasting is rendered obsolete, for we are all recipients of a gift we did not earn.

Truth in Action: Understanding the basis of Ephesians 2:8–9 is crucial, but the transforming power of these verses is fully realized when we internalize them and allow them to shape our daily lives. The truth in these verses challenges our worldview, reshaping our identity and our priorities.

First, these verses dismantle the illusion of self-sufficiency. In a culture that glorifies independence, Ephesians 2:8–9 compels us to acknowledge our profound need for God. Our salvation is not a result of our power or virtue but of a divine rescue mission that humbles us and prompts a posture of gratitude.

Second, these verses foster a spirit of humility. If salvation is a gift and not a wage, then no one can claim superiority or entitlement. We are all equal at the foot of the cross, sinners saved by grace. This insight destroys egotistical barriers and cultivates a culture of respect and humility within the community.

Third, Ephesians 2:8–9 fuels our worship. As we grasp the enormity of God's grace, our hearts are filled with adoration. Our worship is not a transaction to earn God's favor but a response to His unmerited favor He has poured out upon us. It is a melody of gratitude, echoing the psalmist's words, "Give thanks to the Lord, for he is good; his love endures forever" (Psalm 107:1, NIV).

Conclusion: Ephesians 2:8–9 stands as a beacon of light in the landscape of Christianity. It lights the pathway to salvation, revealing that grace is the key that unlocks the door to redemption. As we journey through life, let's embrace these verses as a source of hope, a reminder that our standing before God is not based on our performance but on His unchanging love.

Always remember, that Ephesians 2:8–9 provides a consistent foundation in a world characterized by uncertainty and the never-ending search for affirmation. It invites us to rest in the assurance that our salvation is secure, not because of our accomplishments but because of the unwavering grace of our Heavenly Father. May these verses always speak to our hearts, and inspire a life of faith, humility, and worship as we continue to walk in the unmerited favor of God's grace.

CHAPTER 18

Growing in Grace

> *"Grow in the grace and knowledge of our
> Lord and Savior, Jesus Christ."*
>
> 2 Peter 3:18 NLT

Introduction: In the closing remarks of his second letter, the apostle Peter leaves us with an exhortation that encourages believers to "grow in the grace and knowledge of the Lord and Savior, Jesus Christ." These words are not a suggestion but a directive that invites us into a journey of spiritual maturity, urging us to continually deepen our understanding of God's grace and the character of Jesus Christ. Let's dive into this verse and discover the transformative power of the call to grow in grace.

Growing in Grace: "Grow in grace" is not a one-time event but an ongoing process, a dynamic relationship with the unmerited favor of God. Grace is not merely a theological concept; it's a living, breathing reality that sustains and transforms us. As we navigate the tapestry of our lives, grace is the thread that weaves through our joys and sorrows, victories and defeats. Peter urges us to grow in this grace, to allow it to permeate every aspect of our being.

Grace Beyond Salvation: While the foundational understanding of grace often centers on salvation, Peter challenges us to explore its expansiveness. Salvation is the starting point, the gateway into God's grace, but the journey doesn't end there. Growing in grace means recognizing that every moment is an opportunity to experience God's unmerited favor. It's an acknowledgment that grace is not just a past event but a present reality, shaping our thoughts, actions, and relationships.

The Knowledge of Christ: Peter combines the call to grow in grace with an equally significant mandate—to grow in the knowledge of our Lord and Savior, Jesus Christ. Knowledge here is not a mere intellectual pursuit but a relational depth. It's intimacy with Jesus—the way He loves, forgives, and leads. As we dive into the scriptures, spend time in prayer, and engage in meaningful fellowship, we deepen our knowledge of Christ, unveiling the layers of His character and drawing closer to His heart.

A Continuous Journey: The call to growth is not a stagnant one; it's a continuous journey. Just as a tree grows from a tiny seed to a towering oak, our spiritual growth unfolds gradually. There are seasons of pruning, where God refines and shapes us. There are seasons of abundance where we bear fruit that glorifies Him. In every season, the call remains the same—to grow. It's a call to persevere, to press on, and to trust that the Gardener is orchestrating a beautiful masterpiece with our lives.

Navigating Challenges: Life is filled with challenges, uncertainties, and moments that test our faith. It's in these times that the exhortation to grow in grace and knowledge becomes a lifeline. In the midst of difficulties, grace upholds us by reminding us that God's strength is sufficient to meet our weaknesses. Knowledge empowers us to anchor our faith in the unchanging character of Christ, providing stability when the winds of adversity blow. In the classroom of challenges, we discover that the lessons of grace and the knowledge of Christ are indispensable.

Cultivating a Gracious Heart: Growing in grace extends beyond our personal growth—it spills over into how we relate to others. A heart that has experienced grace becomes a source of love, forgiveness, and compassion. It's a heart that mirrors the grace it has received. As we grow in grace, we become conduits of God's love, extending His favor to those around us. The knowledge of Christ transforms our interactions as we emulate His humility, kindness, and sacrificial love.

A Lifestyle of Worship: To grow in grace and knowledge is, fundamentally, an act of worship. It's a response to the immeasurable love God has lavished upon us through Christ. Our growth becomes an offering—a fragrant aroma rising to the heavens. In our pursuit of grace and knowledge, we declare that God is worthy of our time, attention, and devotion. It's not a checklist of religious duties but a lifestyle that honors the One who first loved us.

Conclusion: As we reflect on Peter's parting words, the depth of their significance becomes apparent. To grow in the grace and knowledge of our Lord and Savior, Jesus Christ, is an invitation to a life of purpose, meaning, and transformation. It's a call to embrace the unmerited favor of God and to continually explore the depths of His character. May this verse resonate in our hearts as a guiding light, propelling us into a journey of lifelong growth—a journey that leads us closer to the heart of God.

CHAPTER 19

In the Potter's Hands

> "This is the word that came to Jeremiah from the LORD:"Go down to the potter's house, and there I will give you, my message."So, I went down to the potter's house, and I saw him working at the wheel.But the pot he was shaping from the clay was marred in his hands; so, the potter formed it into another pot, shaping it as seemed best to him. Then the word of the LORD came to me.He said, "Can I not do with you, Israel, as this potter does?" declares the LORD. "Like clay in the hand of the potter, so are you in my hand, Israel."
>
> JEREMIAH 18:1-6 (NIV)

This verse lets us know that God is not a passive observer in the lives of His children. He actively engages with them, shaping and molding them according to His divine plan.

In the hustle and bustle of life, we often find ourselves caught up in the whirlwind of circumstances, sometimes unable to understand the masterful design being developed by the hands of God, the

Divine Potter. It's in these moments of confusion and uncertainty that we turn to the wisdom of the Scriptures, seeking comfort and guidance. One passage that invites us to consider the artistry of God's hands is found in Jeremiah 18:1–6.

The Setting: A Visit to the Potter's House. The scripture begins with the prophet Jeremiah receiving a divine summons to visit the potter's house. In obedience, he ventures into the workshop, where he becomes a silent observer of this parable. As he watches the skilled potter at his wheel, the Heavenly Father imparts a profound lesson that transcends the boundaries of time and speaks directly to the human soul.

The Potter and the Clay: Divine Sovereignty. Jeremiah beholds the potter shaping a lump of clay into a vessel of his choosing. In this simple yet profound act, we witness a tangible representation of the relationship between the Creator and His creation. The potter's hands move with intention, molding and shaping the clay according to his vision. In the same way, God, as the divine Potter, exercises sovereign authority over our lives.

Jeremiah 18:6 declares, "He said, 'Can I not do with you, Israel, as this potter does?' declares the Lord. 'Like clay in the hand of the potter, so are you in my hand, Israel.'" This verse underscores the truth that God is not a passive observer in the lives of His people. He actively engages with His us, shaping and molding our lives according to His divine plan.

As vessels in the Potter's hands, we may sometimes question the process. Why this shape? Why these circumstances? The answer lies in trusting the wisdom and goodness of the Potter. Proverbs 3:5–6 reminds us, "Trust in the Lord with all your heart and lean not on your own understanding; in all your ways submit to him, and he will make your paths straight."

The Wheel of Circumstances: Divine Transformation. The potter's wheel, a crucial tool in the potter's hands, represents the cyclical nature of life. It spins, turns, and sometimes seems to move in unpredictable ways. In the same way, there are frequent times of happiness, sorrow, success, and challenges in our lives. It is on this spinning wheel of circumstances that God fashions and refines us.

Jeremiah 18:3 describes the clay on the potter's wheel as "marred in his hands." The term "marred" suggests imperfection, flaws, or disruptions in the original design. Similarly, our lives, marked by sin and brokenness, may seem marred and imperfect. Yet, the Potter does not discard the clay; instead, He continues to work on it.

In times of trial and tribulation, when the wheel of our lives seems to spin out of control, we find comfort in the assurance that God is in control. Romans 8:28 reassures us, "And we know that in all things God works for the good of those who love him, who have been called according to his purpose." The Potter's hands, though unseen, are at work, transforming the marred clay of our lives into vessels of beauty and purpose.

The Call to Repentance: Yielding to the Potter's Hands. As the prophet Jeremiah contemplates the potter's house, he is not merely a passive spectator; he becomes a participant in the divine drama. The potter and the clay are not conveying a message of doom but rather one of invitation. It's an invitation to yield, surrender, and allow the Potter's hands to mold us according to His divine plan.

Jeremiah 18:4 states, "But the pot he was shaping from the clay was marred in his hands; so, the potter formed it into another pot, shaping it as seemed best to him." The potter's response to the marred clay is a demonstration of grace and redemption. In the same way, God invites us to repent, acknowledge our imperfections, and allow Him to reshape and renew us.

Repentance is not a one-time event but a continual posture of the heart. It entails a humble acknowledgment of our dependence on God's transforming power and a readiness to submit to His shaping. In the process, we may experience the discomfort of being reshaped, but the end result is a vessel that reflects the beauty and glory of the Potter.

Conclusion: Embracing the Potter's Design. In the quiet intimacy of the potter's house, we find profound lessons. The hands of the divine Potter are not distant or indifferent; they are intimately involved in the shaping of our lives. As vessels on the Potter's wheel, we are called to trust, yield, and embrace the design crafted by the Master Potter.

Let's respond to the call to repentance, acknowledging our need for the Potter's transforming touch. In surrendering to His hands, we find purpose and meaning beyond our understanding. May our lives be characterized by a constant yielding to the hands of our loving Creator, just as the clay yields to the potter's touch.

BUILD

As we live our lives, may we draw inspiration from the prophet Jeremiah and the imagery of the potter's house. In the hands of the Potter, our lives are not mere accidents or random occurrences, but intentional creations designed for a divine purpose. May we trust the hands that shape, transform, and redeem, knowing that we are fearfully and wonderfully made by the skillful hands of the Master Potter.

CHAPTER 20

Living Out the Word

> "Do not merely listen to the word, and so deceive yourselves. Do what it says. Anyone who listens to the word but does not do what it says is like someone who looks at his face in a mirror and, after looking at himself, goes away and immediately forgets what he looks like. But whoever looks intently into the perfect law that gives freedom and continues in it—not forgetting what they have heard but doing it—they will be blessed in what they do."
>
> JAMES 1:22–25 (NIV)

In the book of James, we find practical wisdom and guidance for Christian living. James, the half-brother of Jesus, wrote this letter to encourage believers to live out their faith in tangible ways. This passage of Scripture challenges us to not merely hear the Word of God but to embody it in our daily lives.

James begins with a clear directive: hearing the Word is not enough. Mere listening can lead to self-deception if it doesn't translate into action. It's a caution against passive faith, a faith that stops at hearing without transforming the way we live. In our journey of faith, it's crucial to move beyond the surface of Scripture and allow its truths to penetrate our hearts and guide our actions.

The Deception of Hearing without Doing: James warns against the deception that comes with hearing without doing. It's a sobering reminder that intellectual assent to the teachings of the Bible is insufficient. If we claim to follow Christ but fail to live according to His Word, we deceive ourselves. This self-deception blinds us to the transforming power of God's Word in our lives.

Verse 23–24: Anyone who listens to the word but does not do what it says is like someone who looks at his face in a mirror and, after looking at himself, goes away and immediately forgets what he looks like.

James employs a vivid analogy of a person looking in a mirror. Just as a mirror reflects our physical appearance, the Word of God reflects our spiritual condition. However, if we glance at the mirror of Scripture but promptly forget what we've seen, it's like looking at ourselves in a mirror and promptly forgetting our reflection. This forgetfulness symbolizes a lack of internalizing God's truth.

The Mirror of God's Word: God's Word serves as a mirror, revealing our true selves. It exposes our strengths and weaknesses, our virtues and vices. When we engage with Scripture, it's not merely an intellectual exercise; it's an encounter with the divine mirror that calls us to self-reflection and transformation. The mirror of God's Word shows us who we are and who we can become through Christ.

Verse 25: But whoever looks intently into the perfect law that gives freedom and continues in it—not forgetting what they have heard but doing it—they will be blessed in what they do.

In contrast to the forgetful hearer, James introduces the attentive doer. The key lies in looking intently into the perfect law—the Word of God. It's not a casual glance but a focused, intentional stare that leads to understanding and application. The perfect law, representing God's flawless and liberating truth, is the guide to a blessed life.

The Perfect Law that Gives Freedom: James describes God's Word as the perfect law that gives freedom. In a world that often associates rules and laws with restriction, the idea of a perfect law granting freedom may seem paradoxical. However, in the context of God's Word, it makes perfect sense. The truth found in Scripture doesn't confine us; rather, it liberates us from the bondage of sin and provides a framework for a life of purpose and fulfillment.

Continuing in God's Word: The call to continue in God's Word is an ongoing commitment. It's not a one-time glance, but a lifelong journey of exploration and application. To continue in God's Word requires perseverance, discipline, and a deep desire to align our lives with the principles found in Scripture. It's a daily surrender to the transformative power of God's truth.

Not Forgetting, but Doing: James emphasizes the importance of not forgetting what we have heard but actively doing it. Application is the bridge between hearing and transformation. The blessed life promised in verse 25 is not a result of mere knowledge but of obedience. As we apply God's Word in our lives, we experience the blessings of a life lived in harmony with His principles.

Always remember that James 1:22–25 serves as a powerful reminder of the dynamic relationship between hearing and doing in the Christian life. It challenges us to move beyond a superficial engagement with Scripture and invites us into a transformative journey where the Word of God becomes a mirror, revealing our true selves. As we look intently into this perfect law, not forgetting but doing what it says, we discover the freedom and blessing that come from a life lived in obedience to God's Word. May we be a people who not only hear but actively embody the truth of James 1:22–25, experiencing the richness of a life shaped by the transformative power of God's Word.

CHAPTER 21

More than Conquerors through Christ

> *"Who shall separate us from the love of Christ? Shall trouble, hardship, persecution, famine, nakedness, danger, or a sword? As it is written, "For your sake, we face death all day long; we are considered as sheep to be slaughtered." No, in all these things, we are more than conquerors through him who loved us."*
>
> ROMANS 8:35–37 (NIV)

In Scripture, certain verses stand as timeless pillars, offering comfort and strength to believers navigating the unpredictable currents of life. Romans 8:35–37 is one such passage—a profound declaration of the unyielding love that binds us to Christ and empowers us to overcome every challenge. As we dive into these verses, we begin a journey into the depths of God's love, exploring the inseparable bond that transforms us into triumphant conquerors through Christ.

The Unbreakable Bond of Love: The opening words of Romans 8:35 lay the foundation for our study: "Who shall separate us from the love of Christ?" In posing this rhetorical question, the apostle Paul invites believers to contemplate the nature of the love that Christ has for His followers. The subsequent list of tribulations—trouble, hardship, persecution, famine, nakedness, danger, and sword—presents a comprehensive inventory of life's challenges. Paul paints a vivid picture of a world filled with difficulties, a reality that resonates across time and cultures.

Yet, in the face of such adversities, Paul asserts that none of these circumstances can separate the believer from the love of Christ. The adversities listed are diverse and formidable, representing the full spectrum of human suffering. From the subtle pangs of trouble to the imminent threat of the sword, the apostle highlights the all-encompassing nature of Christ's love. It transcends the temporal and the tangible, reaching into the depths of our souls to provide an unshakeable foundation.

More than Conquerors through Christ: As we move to verse 37, the tone shifts from contemplation to declaration: "No, in all these things, we are more than conquerors through him who loved us." Here, Paul unveils the transforming power of Christ's love. The phrase "more than conquerors" in the original Greek implies a superabundance of victory. It goes beyond merely overcoming; it signifies a resounding triumph that leaves no room for doubt or question. This victory is not achieved in isolation but is tied to the love of Christ.

The source of our conquest is not found in our strength or resilience but in the unwavering love of the One who conquered sin and death on our behalf. Through Christ's sacrificial love, believers are elevated from a posture of mere survival to one of overwhelming victory. The trials that once threatened to separate us from God's love are now transformed into the very arena through which we experience unprecedented triumph.

Understanding the Nature of Conquest: To grasp the magnitude of being "more than conquerors," it's imperative to comprehend the nature of the victory we have in Christ. Our conquest is not characterized by the absence of trials but rather by the transformation of trials into opportunities for God's glory to shine through. The apostle Paul does not present a vision of the Christian life devoid of challenges; instead, he reveals a profound truth—that our response to challenges becomes a testimony to the surpassing power of Christ's love.

In the face of trouble, hardship, and persecution, we are not defeated; rather, we stand as witnesses to the sustaining power of Christ. In times of famine, nakedness, danger, and sword, our triumph is not in evading these challenges but in facing them with unwavering faith, knowing that nothing can separate us from the love of Christ. This perspective radically transforms our understanding of victory, shifting the focus from external circumstances to the internal reality of Christ's love dwelling within us.

The Role of Faith in Conquest: The key to being more than conquerors lies in the realm of faith. Throughout the Bible, faith is portrayed as the catalyst that activates the promises of God. In the context of Romans 8:35–37, faith is the bridge that connects us to the transforming power of Christ's love. It's through faith that we acknowledge the unbreakable bond between us and our Savior, irrespective of external challenges.

Faith empowers believers to view trials not as insurmountable obstacles but as opportunities for God's glory to manifest. It's through faith that we boldly declare our status as conquerors, not because of our might but because of the One who loved us and gave Himself for us. Faith enables us to navigate the ebb and flow of life's tribulations with confidence, knowing that the love of Christ is the constant anchor that secures our victory.

Always remember that Romans 8:35–37 stands as a beacon of hope. These verses provide a resounding affirmation of the enduring love that binds us to Christ in a world filled with trouble, adversity, and persecution. Through the lens of faith, we discover that our triumph is not based on the absence of challenges but on the presence of Christ's love within us.

As more than conquerors, we are not immune to the struggles of life; rather, we are empowered to face them with unwavering confidence in the sufficiency of Christ's love. In moments of famine, nakedness, danger, and sword, our victory is not found in escaping these perils but in the transformative power of Christ's love that sustains us through them.

Allow Romans 8:35–37 to be etched in our hearts as a declaration of our unshakeable position in Christ—a position that transcends circumstances and elevates us to a place of triumph. Let's face life's challenges with the unwavering confidence that, thanks to Christ, we are more than victorious and connected to a love that nothing in all of creation can ever separate us from.

CHAPTER 22

Pressing On Toward the Goal

> *"Not that I have already obtained all this or have already arrived at my goal, but I press on to take hold of that for which Christ Jesus took hold of me."*
>
> — PHILIPPIANS 3:12 (NIV)

In this powerful verse, the apostle Paul shares a profound truth that resonates with every believer on their spiritual journey. It serves as a guiding light, encouraging us to persistently pursue the purpose for which Christ has laid hold of us. As we dive into the richness of Philippians 3:12, we'll uncover layers of wisdom and insight that inspire us to press on in our faith.

Paul humbly acknowledges his own incompleteness. He declares, "Not that I have already obtained all this." Despite his remarkable apostolic ministry, unwavering commitment to Christ, and transforming encounter on the road to Damascus, Paul recognizes the ongoing nature of his spiritual journey. This admission fosters an atmosphere of humility among believers, reminding us that spiritual growth is a continuous process.

The apostle's humility challenges us to resist the temptation of spiritual complacency. It's easy to fall into the trap of thinking that we have "arrived" in our faith, especially during moments of victory or seasons of peace. However, Paul's words echo the truth that our spiritual journey is a lifelong process, a dynamic process of becoming more like Christ. Progress, not perfection, is what defines the journey.

Paul's humility also stands as a counterpoint to any form of self-righteousness. He, who once considered himself blameless according to the law (Philippians 3:6), now acknowledges the need for continual growth. This shift in perspective emphasizes the transforming power of Christ's grace and the sanctifying work of the Holy Spirit in the believer's life.

The phrase "but I press on" encapsulates the essence of Paul's unwavering determination in the face of challenges and uncertainties. The Christian life is not a passive existence; it requires intentional effort and perseverance. "Pressing on" implies a deliberate forward motion, a conscious choice to move closer to the goal set before us. It reflects the idea of running a race with endurance, as described in Hebrews 12:1-2.

Paul's commitment to pressing on is rooted in his understanding of the purpose for which Christ Jesus took hold of him. This purpose transcends personal fulfillment; it is a divine calling and a heavenly goal. The notion of Christ taking hold of us is a beautiful expression of God's initiative in salvation. Before we could reach out to God, He reached out to us through the redemptive work of Jesus Christ.

The purpose for which Christ took hold of Paul, and by extension, every believer, is multi-faceted. It involves conformity to the image of Christ (Romans 8:29), participation in the work of the kingdom, and the glorification of God through a transformed life. Recognizing this purpose adds depth and significance to our journey of faith. It instills a sense of divine intention into the mundane aspects of our lives, reminding us that every experience, trial, and triumph contributes to the unfolding of God's purpose.

The imagery of "taking hold" suggests a divine grasp that is both firm and gentle. Christ doesn't merely seize us; He lovingly holds us in His embrace. This act of taking hold is an act of grace that goes beyond our merit or efforts. It signifies the unmerited favor of God that initiates, sustains, and completes our salvation. As we press on, we do so in the secure knowledge that Christ's grip on us is unyielding and His purposes are unshakable.

Always remember, that Philippians 3:12 serves as a roadmap for the Christian journey. It calls believers to a life of humility, acknowledging our ongoing need for growth. It challenges us to resist the allure of complacency and self-righteousness, fostering a spirit of continuous progression. An understanding of the reason why Christ has taken hold of us motivates us to continue moving forward with vigor.

May this verse be etched in our hearts as a source of encouragement and motivation. Let's continue with the assurance that Jesus, our

Savior, who has called us to a purpose that goes beyond our earthly existence, is guiding us. May the words of Philippians 3:12 echo in our hearts, spurring us forward in our pursuit of the heavenly goal set before us.

CHAPTER 23

Rooted in Trust

> *"They will be like a tree planted by the water that sends out its roots by the stream. It does not fear when heat comes; its leaves are always green. It has no worries in a year of drought and never fails to bear fruit."*
>
> — Jeremiah 17:8 (NIV)

Introduction: In the chaos of our lives, where uncertainty and change are constant, finding a source of unwavering strength becomes crucial. Jeremiah 17:8 offers a profound insight into the essence of a life anchored in trust and faith. Let's go on a journey together into the rich words of this verse, exploring the profound implications it holds for our daily walk with God.

The Verse: Jeremiah 17:8 states, "They will be like a tree planted by the water that sends out its roots by the stream. It does not fear when heat comes; its leaves are always green. It has no worries in a year of drought and never fails to bear fruit."

Planted by the Water: The imagery painted in this verse is vivid and compelling. The tree, firmly planted by the water, serves as a powerful metaphor for the life of a believer deeply rooted in the Word of God. Water, a symbol of life and sustenance, represents the ever-flowing grace and truth that God provides. When our roots extend into the depths of His promises and teachings, we become unshakable.

In our journey of faith, it's essential to continually draw from the well of God's Word. Just as a tree needs water to thrive, we require the spiritual nourishment found in prayer, meditation, and the study of Scripture. The deeper our roots are in God's truth, the more resilient we become in the face of life's challenges.

Fearless in the Heat: Life's challenges often come in the form of scorching heat—difficulties, trials, and unexpected circumstances that threaten to wither our spirits. Yet, the verse assures us that a tree planted by the water does not fear the heat. Likewise, when we are firmly rooted in God's promises, there is no room for fear to take hold.

The promise of God's presence and provision in our lives is a shield against the fears that accompany life's trials. We can face adversity with unwavering confidence, knowing that the living water we are rooted in will sustain us even in the most challenging seasons.

Leaves Always Green: The imagery of evergreen leaves symbolizes a life that remains vibrant and flourishing regardless of external conditions. In a world where circumstances change like shifting sands, the constancy of God's love and faithfulness ensures that our spiritual vitality does not waver.

God's promises are not contingent on our circumstances. The believer's life is characterized by a steadfastness that transcends the temporal, regardless of abundance or scarcity, joy or sorrow. The assurance that our leaves will always be green is a testament to the enduring nature of God's grace.

No Worries in a Year of Drought: Droughts are inevitable in life—seasons of scarcity, loss, or hardship. However, the promise of Jeremiah 17:8 offers comfort in the face of such challenges. A life deeply rooted in God's Word does not succumb to anxiety and worry when resources seem scarce.

The world may face droughts of various kinds, but the believer, rooted in the abundance of God's promises, remains secure. Trusting in God's provision allows us to navigate seasons of lack with a confident expectation that our needs will be met according to His riches in glory.

Never Fails to Bear Fruit: The ultimate purpose of a tree is to bear fruit, and the same holds true for our lives as believers. The promise that a tree planted by the water never fails to bear fruit reminds us of the transforming power of a life grounded in faith.

The fruits of the Spirit—love, joy, peace, patience, kindness, goodness, faithfulness, gentleness, and self-control (Galatians 5:22–23)—are the natural outcome of a life rooted in God's Word. As we abide in Him, we find the strength to impact the world around us positively.

Always remember, Jeremiah 17:8 details the essence of a life deeply rooted in trust and faith in God. It calls us to be like the tree planted by the water, drawing our strength, sustenance, and identity from the eternal well of God's Word. In a world where uncertainties abound, this verse stands as a beacon of hope, assuring us that a life anchored in God's promises remains unshaken, resilient, and fruitful.

As we meditate on Jeremiah 17:8, may it inspire us to cultivate a life of trust, to deepen our roots in the soil of God's truth, and to bear the fruit that glorifies Him. May we be like trees, flourishing by the water, undeterred by life's heat, and evergreen in the assurance of God's unwavering love and provision.

CHAPTER 24

Soaring on Wings of Faith

> *"But those who trust in the Lord will find new strength. They will soar high on wings like eagles. They will run and not grow weary. They will walk and not faint."*
>
> Isaiah 40:31 (NLT)

These words spoken by Isaiah offer comfort and inspiration. In this devotion, we will dive into the richness of Isaiah 40:31, exploring the profound promises it holds for those who place their trust in the Lord.

The verse begins with a powerful declaration: "But those who trust in the Lord will find new strength." Trust is the cornerstone of our relationship with God. The invitation to put our trust in the Lord is a call to embrace our Heavenly Father's unwavering faithfulness in a world full of uncertainty. Trust is not a passive, but an active reliance on the One who holds the universe in His hands. As we trust, we tap into a divine source of strength, an unending reservoir that breathes new life into our weary hearts.

The imagery that follows is both vivid and compelling: "They will soar high on wings like eagles." Eagles are majestic creatures known for their strength, keen vision, and ability to soar to great heights. In likening our spiritual journey to the soaring flight of eagles, Isaiah paints a picture of the boundless possibilities that unfold when we trust in God. Just as eagles navigate the skies with grace and purpose, those who trust in the Lord can rise above life's challenges, gaining a heavenly perspective that transcends the limitations of circumstance.

Soaring on wings like eagles also speaks to a freedom that transcends the constraints of earthly concerns. It symbolizes a release from the burdens that weigh us down—whether they be doubts, fears, or the weariness of life's demands. God's promise isn't just that we'll survive; it's that we'll overcome thanks to a supernatural strength that gives us the fortitude and resiliency to face each day.

The verse continues: "They will run and not grow weary. They will walk and not faint." The progression from running to walking suggests a journey, in which we are not only sustained but propelled forward by the strength derived from trusting in God. In the race of life, where challenges can be relentless and obstacles seem insurmountable, the promise is that our steps will not falter and our energy will not decrease, for we draw from a wellspring of divine endurance.

BUILD

This promise is not a guarantee of a trouble-free existence but an assurance that, even in the midst of trials, we will not succumb to weariness. It speaks to the resilience born out of trust—the kind of endurance that is sustained by a deep connection with the source of all strength. In the face of life's demands, we are not left to rely on our own limited resources; instead, we are invited to tap into the infinite power of the Almighty.

Consider the implications of this promise in the context of your own life. Perhaps you are facing challenges that seem insurmountable, or the demands of daily life have left you feeling weary and worn. The invitation is clear: trust in the Lord. As you surrender your burdens and uncertainties to Him, you open the door to a renewed strength that transcends human understanding.

In times of waiting, when answers seem elusive and the future uncertain, the promise of Isaiah 40:31 is a beacon of hope. It reminds us that, in the quiet trust of waiting, God is at work, renewing our strength and preparing us for the journey ahead. Like a patient eagle waiting for the perfect current to soar upon, our waiting is not in vain. It is a sacred space where our trust deepens and our strength is quietly renewed.

Consider the transforming power of soaring on wings like eagles. In the height of God's presence, our perspective changes. The challenges that once seemed insurmountable became growth opportunities. The storms that threatened to overwhelm are seen from a vantage point of peace. As we rise above the noise and distractions of life, we gain clarity, insight, and a renewed sense of purpose. The promise of soaring is an invitation to embrace a perspective that transcends the temporal and aligns with the eternal.

So, how do we practically apply the truths found in Isaiah 40:31 to our lives? It begins with trust—a deliberate choice to place our confidence in God's unwavering faithfulness. Trust is not a one-time decision but a daily surrender, a continuous reliance on the One who holds our past, present, and future in His hands. As we trust, we open ourselves to the transforming work of God, allowing Him to renew our strength and empower us to soar on wings like eagles.

Prayer becomes the conduit through which our trust is expressed. In prayer, we lay our burdens before God, acknowledging our need for His strength. We pour out our hearts, sharing our hopes, fears, and dreams with the One who cares deeply for us. In the intimate space of communion with God, trust grows, and our souls find rest in His presence.

Reading and meditating on God's Word is another essential aspect of cultivating trust. The Bible is a reservoir of promises, wisdom, and encouragement. As we immerse ourselves in Scripture, we discover the character of God, His faithfulness in the lives of those who have gone before us, and the unchanging nature of His promises. The more we meditate on God's Word, the more our trust in Him deepens, providing a solid foundation for the journey ahead.

Community is also crucial in our journey of trust. Surrounding ourselves with fellow believers who encourage, uplift, and challenge us strengthens our faith. Together, we can remind each other of God's promises, share testimonies of His faithfulness, and provide support in times of need. The body of believers becomes a tangible expression of God's love, a reminder that we do not walk this journey alone.

Always remember, Isaiah 40:31 is a timeless and powerful promise that invites us to trust in the Lord, to find new strength, and to soar on wings like eagles. As we navigate the complexities of life, let's anchor our souls in the unwavering faithfulness of our God. May we choose daily to trust in Him, to surrender our burdens in prayer, to immerse ourselves in His Word, and to walk in community with fellow believers. In doing so, we open ourselves to the transformative work of God, allowing Him to renew our strength and empower us to soar to new heights in our journey of faith.

CHAPTER 25

The Cornerstone of Faith

> "For in Scripture it says: "See, I lay a stone in Zion, a chosen and precious cornerstone, and the one who trusts in him will never be put to shame." Now to you who believe, this stone is precious. But to those who do not believe, "The stone the builders rejected has become the cornerstone,"
>
> 1 PETER 2:6-7 (NIV)

Introduction: In the spiritual journey of life, the foundation upon which we build our life is very important. In 1 Peter 2:6-7, the apostle Peter draws upon the imagery of a cornerstone—a chosen and precious stone in Zion. This cornerstone is none other than Jesus Christ, and the way we respond to Him shapes the very essence of our faith and, consequently, the life we construct.

The Chosen and Precious Cornerstone: The metaphor of a cornerstone holds rich significance in biblical imagery. In ancient construction practices, the cornerstone was the principal stone placed at the corner of a building. It determined the alignment and stability of the entire structure. In this passage, Peter proclaims Jesus as the chosen and precious cornerstone. This declaration echoes the prophecies of the Old Testament, particularly in Isaiah 28:16, where God declares, "See, I lay a stone in Zion, a tested stone, a precious cornerstone for a sure foundation."

Jesus, the cornerstone, is not chosen arbitrarily but is divinely appointed. He is the foundation upon which God builds His redemptive plan for humanity. In God's sovereign design, Jesus is the cornerstone around which our lives are meant to revolve.

Building a Life of Trust: The passage goes on to assure believers that those who trust in this precious cornerstone will never be put to shame. Trust is the key that unlocks the transforming power of Christ in our lives. It involves surrendering our plans, fears, and ambitions to the One who is both the architect and builder of our faith journey.

Trusting in Christ means acknowledging His lordship over every aspect of our lives. It means allowing His teachings, exemplified in His life and recorded in Scripture, to guide our decisions, shape our character, and define our purpose. As we build our lives on the sure foundation of Jesus, our trust becomes an unshakable confidence in His faithfulness, goodness, and love.

The Rejected Cornerstone: However, not everyone recognizes the value of this cornerstone. Peter reminds us that, to those who do not believe, "The stone the builders rejected has become the cornerstone." Rejecting Christ is not new. Throughout history, people have dismissed and denied Him. Yet, in the divine economy, rejection does not diminish His significance; rather, it magnifies His redemptive power.

The rejection of Christ, foretold in Psalm 118:22, becomes a pivotal moment in the unfolding drama of salvation. The very stone that some deem unsuitable for their construction projects becomes the cornerstone—the very thing holding together God's grand design for humanity.

The Preciousness of Christ: For those who believe, Peter emphasizes the preciousness of this cornerstone. The word "precious" conveys the idea of great value, rarity, and uniqueness. In a world where values and priorities often shift like sand, Christ stands as the unwavering standard of truth, love, and righteousness. The unchanging nature of God Himself determines His preciousness, not popular opinion or cultural trends.

Recognizing the preciousness of Christ calls for a recalibration of our affections and priorities. It prompts us to evaluate what we deem valuable in the light of eternity. The pursuit of worldly success, material wealth, and temporal pleasures pales in comparison to the immeasurable worth of knowing and following Christ. He is the treasure hidden in the field, the pearl of great price, and to those who understand His preciousness, no sacrifice is too great to obtain Him.

Conclusion: In conclusion, 1 Peter 2:6-7 beckons us to examine the foundation upon which we are building our lives. Jesus Christ, the chosen and precious cornerstone, invites us to trust Him completely.

As we place our confidence in Him, our lives become testimonies to His faithfulness, grace, and transforming power.

The rejected cornerstone has become the cornerstone of our faith. In a world that often rejects the values of the Kingdom, we are called to stand firm, building our lives on the unshakable foundation of Christ. May we, as believers, recognize the preciousness of Jesus and build lives that reflect His glory, drawing others to the sure foundation that is found in Him alone.

CHAPTER 26

The Rock of My Salvation

> *"The Lord is my rock, my fortress, and my savior; my God is my rock, in whom I find protection. He is my shield, the power that saves me, and my place of safety."*
>
> — Psalm 18:2 (NLT)

Introduction: In life, filled with joy and sorrow, triumphs and trials, we often find ourselves standing at the crossroads of uncertainty. It is in these moments that we yearn for a stable foundation, a refuge that withstands the storms of life. Psalm 18:2 beautifully encapsulates this longing, "The Lord is my rock, my fortress, and my savior; my God is my rock, in whom I find protection. He is my shield, the power that saves me, and my place of safety."

The Lord as a Rock: The metaphor of God as a rock is profound and rich with significance. In a world filled with shifting sands and ever-changing circumstances, God stands as an immovable and unshakeable rock. He is unaffected by adverse circumstances. When the storms of life threaten to sweep us away, we can find solace in the stability of our Rock.

Consider the strength of a solid rock—unyielding to external pressures and resilient in the face of adversity. Likewise, our God is a steadfast foundation, a firm ground upon which we can stand with confidence. When the challenges of life threaten to overwhelm us, we can find refuge in the unchanging nature of our God.

My Fortress and Savior: The psalmist further describes God as a fortress and a savior. A fortress is a place of safety, a stronghold that protects from external threats. In times of danger, we can run to God, our fortress, and find safety and security under His wings.

Our God not only provides a safe haven but is also our Savior. He rescues us from the snares of sin, the clutches of despair, and the grip of hopelessness. In moments of weakness, when our strength fails us, God becomes our strength. He is the One who lifts us from the miry clay, setting our feet upon the solid ground of His grace.

My Shield and Place of Safety: The imagery of God as a shield speaks of His protective nature. In the midst of life's battles, He shields us from the arrows of doubt, the spears of fear, and the onslaught of the enemy. As a shield, God not only defends but also deflects the blows that come our way.

In addition, God is our place of safety. In a world where danger lurks around every corner, we can find safety in the arms of the Almighty.

It is in His presence that we discover true security—a safety that transcends the physical and extends into the depths of our souls.

The Power That Saves: The psalmist acknowledges that God is not just a passive observer in our lives. He is the power that saves us. When sin ensnares us and guilt weighs heavily on our hearts, God's power intervenes and frees us. His saving power extends to every part of our lives—spiritual, emotional, and physical.

God's power is limitless and infinite; it is not subject to human limitations. When we feel weak and powerless, His strength is made perfect in our weakness (2 Corinthians 12:9). As we surrender to His power, we find that it is sufficient to carry us through the trials we face.

Conclusion: Psalm 18:2 paints a vivid picture of our relationship with God. He is not distant and indifferent to our struggles. Instead, He is our Rock, our Fortress, and our Savior. In Him, we find stability, protection, and deliverance. The beauty of this psalm lies in its reminder that our God is not a passive observer but an active participant in our lives, providing strength, protection, and salvation.

As we navigate the unpredictable journey of life, let's anchor our faith in the Rock that does not waver. Let's seek refuge in the fortress that cannot be breached. May we find comfort in the saving power of our God, who is not only our shield but also our place of safety. In every trial and triumph, let the words of Psalm 18:2 resound in our hearts, a declaration of our unshakable trust in the Lord, our Rock and Redeemer.

CHAPTER 27

The Sure Foundation

> *"Therefore thus says the Lord God: 'Behold, I lay in Zion a stone for a foundation, A tried stone, a precious cornerstone, a sure foundation; Whoever believes will not act hastily'"*
>
> ISAIAH 28:16 (NKJV)

Introduction: In all of Scripture, certain verses stand out as beacons of profound truth, casting their light over our lives. Isaiah 28:16 is one such verse that resonates with significance. It unveils a promise that transcends the temporal and offers a foundation upon which the very fabric of our faith is woven. Let's dive into Isaiah 28:16 and explore the rich layers of meaning and the enduring relevance it holds for believers today.

The Context of Isaiah 28: Isaiah, often referred to as the "prophet of redemption," delivered his messages to the southern kingdom of Judah during a period of political instability and spiritual declension. The people had strayed from the ways of God, and the consequences of their disobedience were looming on the horizon. In Isaiah 28, the prophet addresses the northern kingdom of Israel's impending judgment, portraying the spiritual stupor of the people.

The verse in focus, Isaiah 28:16, emerges in the midst of Isaiah's rebuke and warning. The Lord, through the prophet, announces a cornerstone—a foundation that stands in stark contrast to the shaky alliances and flawed strategies of the people. This cornerstone, as we will discover, finds its ultimate fulfillment in the person of Jesus Christ.

The Cornerstone: A Symbol of Stability and Significance

Isaiah 28:16 declares, "Therefore thus says the Lord God: 'Behold, I lay in Zion a stone for a foundation, a tried stone, a precious cornerstone, a sure foundation; Whoever believes will not act hastily'" (NKJV). In this proclamation, God unveils a metaphorical cornerstone—a stone of foundational significance and unwavering stability.

In the ancient world, the cornerstone held pivotal importance in construction. It was the first stone laid, serving as a reference point for the alignment and integrity of the entire structure. This cornerstone in Isaiah's metaphor is none other than the divine foundation that God Himself laid in Zion, the city of David. This cornerstone is characterized by three essential attributes.

1. **Tried Stone**: The cornerstone is not hastily chosen or untested. It has endured trials and emerged unscathed,

demonstrating its reliability. This attribute echoes the proven faithfulness of God throughout history. His promises are not hollow; they have withstood the test of time and circumstance.

2. **Precious Cornerstone**: The value of this cornerstone is immeasurable. It is not a common stone but one of unique and unparalleled significance. In the grand narrative of redemption, Jesus Christ is the precious cornerstone—the embodiment of God's love and the foundation of salvation.

3. **Sure Foundation**: The cornerstone serves as the bedrock of the entire structure. It ensures stability and durability. Likewise, God's foundation in Christ provides a sure and unshakable basis for our faith. Amidst the shifting sands of life, this foundation remains steadfast.

The Fulfillment in Christ: As we navigate the New Testament, the curtains of revelation are drawn back to reveal the ultimate fulfillment of Isaiah's prophecy in the person of Jesus Christ. The apostle Peter, drawing from Isaiah 28:16, affirms this in 1 Peter 2:6, stating, "Therefore it is also contained in the Scripture, 'Behold, I lay in Zion a chief cornerstone, elect, precious, and he who believes in Him will by no means be put to shame'" (NKJV).

Jesus, the Chief Cornerstone, is the embodiment of the tried stone, the precious cornerstone, and the sure foundation foretold by Isaiah. In Ephesians 2:20, Paul reinforces this truth, describing believers as being "built on the foundation of the apostles and prophets, Jesus Christ Himself being the chief cornerstone"

(NKJV). The entire edifice of the Christian faith rests on the person and work of Christ.

Application to Our Lives: Isaiah 28:16, though written centuries ago, reverberates with relevance for believers today. As we grapple with the complexities of life, this verse offers profound insights that resonate across the corridors of time.

1. **Stability in a Shifting World:** The cornerstone of Christ provides a stable anchor in the tumultuous seas of life. Believers can find comfort in the unchanging nature of Christ in a world characterized by uncertainty, political unrest, and personal difficulties.

2. **Value in Christ's Sacrifice:** The preciousness of the cornerstone underscores the immeasurable value of Christ's sacrifice. In a culture that often assigns worth based on external achievements or possessions, the believer finds their true significance in the redemptive work of the cross.

3. **Confidence in God's Promises:** The tried stone reminds us that God's promises are not empty words. They have endured the tests of time and remain steadfast. As we encounter trials and tribulations, we can rest in the assurance that God is faithful to His Word.

4. **Building a Life on the Sure Foundation:** Isaiah 28:16 challenges us to build our lives on the sure foundation of Christ. This involves aligning our values, priorities, and

choices with the teachings of Scripture. As we do so, we construct a life that withstands the storms of adversity.

Conclusion: Isaiah 28:16 encourages us to look upon the cornerstone laid in Zion—a cornerstone that finds its fulfillment in Jesus Christ. As believers, we are firmly rooted in the tried and priceless cornerstone of God's promises. In Christ, we discover stability, significance, and the unwavering assurance that our faith rests on a sure foundation. May this truth resonate in our hearts, shaping our lives and guiding us through the ever-changing currents of existence.

CHAPTER 28

The Unfailing Promise of God

> *"The Lord will perfect that which concerns me; Your mercy, O Lord, endures forever; do not forsake the works of Your hands."*
>
> PSALM 138:8 (NKJV)

Many of us remember Billy Graham, the most popular American preacher of the 20th century.

He once shared a story about his wife, Ruth, who was driving through a construction zone for many miles on a highway. After carefully following the detours and warning signs, she finally came to the last sign that read: "End of the construction zone. Thank you for your patience."

Struck by the message, she went home and told Billy she wanted that line engraved on her tombstone: "End of construction. Thank you for your patience."

Introduction: Psalm 138:8 is a beacon of hope, a verse that encourages us to dive into the depths of God's unwavering commitment to His children.

This single verse proclaims the profound truths about the nature of our relationship with God, offering comfort to the weary and assurance to the doubtful. Let's take a journey through Psalm 138:8 and uncover the promises and revelations it holds for those who seek the heart of God.

The Lord Will Perfect: "The Lord will perfect..." These words are a promise directly from God. God's dedication to resolving the concerns of His children serves as an anchor for our souls in a world filled with flaws and uncertainty. The term "perfect" here conveys the idea of bringing to completion or fulfilling that which is lacking.

Consider your own life—the dreams, the challenges, and the uncertainties that cloud the horizon. There may be loose ends, unfinished patterns, and incomplete designs. Yet, the psalmist declares with confidence that the Lord will perfect all that concerns you. This assurance is not based on our merit or performance but is grounded in the unchanging character of God.

It's a promise that echoes throughout Scripture, that resonates in Paul's words to the Philippians: "Being confident of this very thing, that He who has begun a good work in you will complete it until the day of Jesus Christ" (Philippians 1:6, NKJV). The God who initiated the work of transformation in your life is faithful to bring it to fruition.

Your Mercy, O Lord, Endures Forever: As we go deeper into Psalm 138:8, we encounter a pivotal truth—the enduring mercy of the Lord. In life's challenges, it's easy to lose sight of God's mercy and to forget the depth of His compassion and grace. Yet the psalmist encourages us to remember and anchor our faith in the unchanging nature of God's mercy.

The word "mercy" carries significance in Scripture. It is not a fleeting emotion or a temporary sentiment. Instead, it is an integral aspect of God's character, an unshakable foundation upon which our relationship with Him is built. His mercy is not subject to circumstances or human emotions. It endures. It's steadfast. It's unwavering. And, it's eternal.

In our moments of weakness, when we stumble, it's the enduring mercy of the Lord that lifts us from the depths of despair. It's His mercy that extends a lifeline to the broken and humble in heart, inviting us into the embrace of forgiveness and restoration. As the psalmist affirms, this mercy endures forever—a truth that transcends the limitations of time and extends into eternity.

Do Not Forsake the Works of Your Hands: The final plea in Psalm 138:8 is a heartfelt cry: "Do not forsake the works of Your hands." In this petition, is a recognition of our frailty and a humble acknowledgment of our dependence on the sustaining power of God. We are the works of His hands—crafted, molded, and intricately formed by the Creator of the universe, our Heavenly Father.

The plea is not born out of doubt but is a fervent expression of reliance on God's faithfulness. It's a recognition that our journey, our transformation, and our destiny are linked to the divine craftsmanship of the Almighty. The hands that formed us will not abandon us. The One who began the good work will bring it to completion.

This plea speaks to the sentiments of other psalms, such as Psalm 139, where the psalmist marvels at the intimate knowledge and care of God: "For You formed my inward parts; You covered me in my mother's womb" (Psalm 139:13, NKJV). The assurance that God will not forsake the works of His hands resonates with the truth that we are held in the palm of His hand, and secure in the love that surpasses all understanding.

Application in Daily Life: How do we apply the truths of Psalm 138:8 to our daily lives? In the hustle and bustle of our routines, in the face of trials and tribulations, we are invited to anchor our faith in the promises of this psalm.

1. **Surrender Control**: Recognize that the Lord is at work in your life, perfecting that which concerns you. Release the grip of control and trust in His sovereign plan.

2. **Remember His Mercy**: In moments of failure and shortcomings, remember the enduring mercy of the Lord. Approach His throne with confidence, knowing that His mercy is a fountain that never runs dry.

3. **Pray with Confidence**: Approach God with boldness in prayer, knowing that He will not forsake the works of His hands. Your prayers are heard, and God is actively involved in every detail of your life.

4. **Live in Assurance**: Walk in the assurance that the God who began a good work in you will bring it to completion. Let this truth shape your identity and influence your response to the challenges you face.

In conclusion, always remember, that Psalm 138:8 invites us to place our trust in the unfailing promises of God. As we meditate on these words, our hearts be stirred with a renewed sense of faith, and our lives will be a testimony to the perfecting work of the Lord, the enduring mercy that sustains us, and the unwavering commitment of the God who holds us in the palm of His hands.

CHAPTER 29

The Wise Builder

> "Therefore, everyone who hears these words of mine and puts them into practice is like a wise man who built his house on the rock. The rain came down, the streams rose, and the winds blew and beat against that house, yet it did not fall because it had its foundation on the rock. But everyone who hears these words of mine and does not put them into practice is like a foolish man who built his house on sand. The rain came down, the streams rose, and the winds blew and beat against that house, and it fell with a great crash."
>
> Matthew 7:24–27 (NIV)

In these verses, Jesus imparts a powerful lesson through a simple yet vivid analogy of two builders—one wise and the other foolish. This lesson transcends the physical act of constructing houses and delves into the spiritual realm, emphasizing the importance of a strong and enduring foundation for our faith.

The Wise Builder: The wise builder in this parable is someone who not only hears the teachings of Jesus but also puts them into practice. Their actions reflect their commitment to Christ's words, making them comparable to a person who constructs their house on a solid rock. Building on a rock signifies a secure and immovable foundation capable of withstanding the fiercest storms of life.

As followers of Christ, we are called to be like the wise builder. We must not only listen to the teachings of our Lord but also live them out daily. It is not enough to be hearers of the Word; we must be doers as well (James 1:22). Our faith, like a house built on a rock, should remain firm and unshakable, even when life's challenges come crashing down upon us.

The Unwavering Foundation: The rock on which the wise builder's house is constructed symbolizes Jesus Christ Himself. He is the unshakable foundation on which we should build our lives. When our faith is rooted in Him, we are assured of its stability. Regardless of the storms that rage against us—sickness, financial difficulties, broken relationships, or any other trials—our foundation remains steadfast.

Jesus promises that those who build their lives on Him will not be swept away by the adversities of life. He is our refuge, our strength, and our deliverer (Psalm 46:1). Through Him, we find strength to endure, courage to persevere, and hope for the future. The foundation of our faith in Christ is what enables us to stand tall even in the face of life's most challenging circumstances.

The Foolish Builder: On the other hand, the foolish builder represents those who hear the teachings of Jesus but do not put them into practice. They construct their lives on a foundation of sand—a symbol of instability and weakness. When the storms of life come, their faith crumbles, and they experience a great fall.

This is a sobering reminder of the consequences of mere intellectual assent to the gospel without genuine surrender and obedience to Christ. Merely listening to the Word without putting it into practice is akin to building one's house on shifting sand. Inevitably, when life's trials and tribulations assail us, our faith will prove fragile and unreliable.

The Crash of Unbelief: The parable concludes with a vivid image: the house built on sand falls with a great crash. The crash represents the ultimate collapse of a life that is built on unbelief and disobedience. Such a life may appear sturdy for a time, but when the storms of life intensify, its true foundation—or lack thereof—is exposed.

For those who do not heed Jesus' teachings, the spiritual crash can result in a life marred by despair, doubt, and disillusionment. Their lack of a solid foundation in Christ leads to a loss of hope and direction. This is a dire warning to all who hear the gospel but do not act upon it.

Practical Application: To fully embrace the wisdom in this parable, we must evaluate our own lives as builders. Are we constructing our faith on the rock, or are we building on shifting sands? Here are some practical steps we can take to ensure that we are wise builders:

1. Study the Word: Devote time to studying the teachings of Jesus and the entire Bible. Knowledge of God's Word is essential for building a strong foundation.

2. Apply the Word: It is not enough to merely learn Scripture; we must put it into practice. Live out the principles and values taught by Jesus in your daily life.

3. Seek a Personal Relationship with Christ: Building your life on Jesus Christ, the rock, begins with a personal relationship with Him. This relationship is nurtured through prayer, worship, and fellowship with other believers.

4. Trust in God's Promises: In times of trial and testing, lean on God's promises. His Word is a source of strength and encouragement when we face life's storms.

5. Accountability: Surround yourself with fellow believers who can hold you accountable in your walk of faith. This will help you remain steadfast and committed to building on the rock.

Always remember, the parable of the wise and foolish builders in Matthew 7:24–27 serves as a reminder of the significance of a strong foundation in Christ. It challenges us to be not just hearers of the Word but doers as well, for it is in the application of Christ's teachings that our faith becomes unshakable. May we, like the wise builder, build our lives upon the solid rock of Jesus Christ and stand firm through every storm that life brings our way.

CHAPTER 30

Unchanging

> *"Jesus Christ is the same yesterday, today, and forever."*
> HEBREWS 13:8 (NIV)

Introduction: Hebrews 13:8 is a powerful and reassuring verse, that stands as a point of hope for all believers. The author emphasizes Christ's unwavering consistency in a world characterized by change and unpredictability.

Yesterday: The opening words, "Jesus Christ is the same yesterday," take us back to the beginning of time, reminding us that Christ's nature has been constant throughout history. In a world where societies rise and fall, and cultures change, Christ remains an unchanging, steadfast anchor. As we reflect on the yesterdays of our lives, with their triumphs and tribulations, we find comfort in knowing that the Savior who walked beside us then is the same Savior who walks with us today.

In the Old Testament, we encounter glimpses of the pre-incarnate Christ—the God who appeared to Abraham, wrestled with Jacob, and spoke through the prophets. In these manifestations, we witness the enduring love and faithfulness that find their ultimate expression in the person of Jesus Christ. The promises made in ancient times find their fulfillment in Him, reinforcing the fact that He is the unchanging thread woven through the tapestry of human history.

Today: The second part of the verse declares, "And today," a reminder that Christ's constancy is not confined to history but is a present reality. In the hustle and bustle of our contemporary lives, where uncertainty looms and the ground beneath us seems ever shifting, the assurance that Jesus Christ remains the same offers unparalleled comfort.

In a world where trends change with the blink of an eye and the pursuit of the latest and greatest consumes many, the constancy of Christ becomes a counter-cultural declaration. His teachings in the Scriptures provide a timeless and unchanging guide for navigating the complexities of today. The moral and spiritual compass found in Christ's words remains as relevant now as it was when first uttered, offering a stable foundation in a world often characterized by moral relativism.

As we face the challenges of today—be they personal struggles, societal unrest, or global crises—the unchanging nature of Christ encourages us to find our refuge in Him. In a culture that often glorifies the fleeting and the temporary, we can rest assured that our Savior is an anchor for the soul, firm and secure (Hebrews 6:19).

Forever: The concluding part of the verse encapsulates the eternal truth that Jesus Christ is the same "forever." This proclamation transcends the boundaries of time, offering a glimpse into the future and the assurance that, regardless of what may come, Christ will remain constant. It's a promise that extends beyond the temporal confines of our earthly existence, reaching into the eternity that awaits believers.

The promise of an unchanging Savior is a source of enduring hope in a world where change is inevitable and the future is uncertain. The challenges of life, the trials that test our faith, and the inevitability of our mortal journey all find their context in the light of eternity. In Christ's unchanging nature, we discover a hope that goes beyond the transient nature of this world, anchoring us in the certainty of His promises.

Implications for Our Lives: Hebrews 13:8 is not merely a theological statement; it's a profound truth with practical implications for our daily lives. The unchanging nature of Christ invites us into a relationship characterized by faith, submission, and a strong sense of security.

1. **Trust in the Unchanging Savior:** In a world that often disappoints and where trust is a scarce commodity, the constancy of Christ becomes a foundation on which we can build our trust. Our Savior does not vacillate or alter His promises based on circumstances; He is faithful yesterday, today, and forever. As we navigate the uncertainties of life, we can trust in His unchanging character.

2. **Obedience to Timeless Truths:** The unchanging nature of Christ's teachings challenges us to embrace timeless truths that transcend cultural shifts and societal trends. In a world that frequently redefines morality and truth, the unchanging Word of God provides a moral compass by which we can navigate the complexities of today.

3. **Security in an Uncertain World: In a world where instability is prevalent, Christ's unchanging nature offers a profound sense of security.** Economic fluctuations, political unrest, and personal crises may threaten to shake the foundations of our lives, but in Christ, we find an unshakable anchor. Our security is not rooted in the temporal but in the eternal.

Conclusion: Hebrews 13:8 is a timeless declaration that echoes and reverberates in the hearts of believers today. It encapsulates the essence of who Jesus Christ is—unchanging, constant, and eternal. In a world that is ever-changing, Christ's constancy stands as a beacon of hope, inviting us to trust in Him, obey His timeless truths, and find security in the unchanging Savior.

As we meditate on this verse, let's allow its truth to permeate every aspect of our lives. May we find comfort in the unchanging nature of Christ's love, draw strength from His unwavering faithfulness, and live in the light of the eternal promises that He, the same yesterday, today, and forever, has graciously bestowed upon us.

CHAPTER 31

We Are God's Field and Building

"For we are God's fellow workers; you are God's field, God's building. According to the grace of God which was given to me, like a wise master builder, I laid a foundation, and another is building on it. But each person must be careful how he builds on it. For no one can lay a foundation other than the one which is laid, which is Jesus Christ. Now if any person builds on the foundation with gold, silver, precious stones, wood, hay, and straw, each one's work will become evident; for the day will show it because it is to be revealed with fire, and the fire itself will test the quality of each person's work. If any person's work which he has built on it remains, he will receive a reward. If any person's work is burned up, he will suffer loss, but he himself will be saved, yet only as through fire."

1 Corinthians 3:9–15 (NASB)

In these verses, the Apostle Paul uses the imagery of construction to convey profound spiritual truths. He addresses the Corinthians, reminding them that they are God's field and God's building.

Paul, in his role as a wise master builder, lays a foundation, and he declares that there can be no other foundation but Jesus Christ. This foundation is solid and unshakable, and it is the starting point for every believer's spiritual journey. As Christians, our lives are built upon the bedrock of Christ, and the choices we make in constructing our spiritual houses matter.

Paul goes on to describe the different materials used in building on this foundation—gold, silver, precious stones, wood, hay, and straw. These materials represent the quality of our actions, attitudes, and works in our Christian life. Some are long-lasting and symbolic of gold, silver, and precious stones, while others are transient and symbolic of wood, hay, and straw.

The apostle's metaphor suggests that our lives are like construction projects, and every day we are adding to the structure. The choices we make, the way we treat others, our commitment to prayer and studying God's Word—these are the building materials we use. Are we building with durable materials that will withstand the test of time and adversity, or are we using materials that the fires of life's difficulties will consume?

The pivotal moment arrives when the day shows the work's true nature through fire. The fire symbolizes the refining process that reveals the quality of our deeds and motives. This refining fire can take various forms—challenges, hardships, and trials that test the strength and endurance of our faith. In those moments, the true nature of our spiritual construction becomes evident.

The outcome is twofold. If our work endures the fire, we receive a reward. This reward is not just a prize for good behavior but a reflection of a life lived in accordance with God's will. It's the result of faithfulness, obedience, and a genuine love for God and others. On the other hand, we suffer loss if the flames consume our work. However, the comforting truth is that even in the midst of loss, the believer is saved. Salvation remains secure, but the rewards that could have been received are forfeited.

This passage challenges us to evaluate the choices we make in our daily lives. What materials are we using to build our spiritual houses? Are we investing in eternal values, or are we preoccupied with the transient and temporary? It calls us to examine the motives behind our actions to ensure that we are building with a sincere desire to honor and glorify God rather than seeking self-gratification.

In addition, it prompts us to consider the refining process. Do we shy away from challenges and difficulties, or do we recognize them as opportunities for growth and refinement? The fire of trials may be uncomfortable, but it is in those moments that our faith is tested, refined, and ultimately strengthened.

In conclusion, 1 Corinthians 3:9–15 serves as a profound reminder that our lives are under construction. We are not passive observers but active participants in the building process. Christ is our foundation, and every choice we make adds to the structure. Let's be intentional in our construction, using materials that endure the refining fire, and may our ultimate goal be the reward that comes from a life lived for the glory of God.

Build Your Life on the Sure Foundation
Receive Jesus as Your Personal Savior

The most important relationship for every one of us is our relationship with Jesus Christ. Choosing to believe that he is who he claimed to be—the Son of God and the only way to salvation—and receiving him by faith as your Lord and Savior is the most vital act anyone will ever do. We want life. He is life. We need cleansing. He is the living water.

If you have not yet given your life to Jesus and would like to invite him into your life, here is a simple prayer for you to pray:

Jesus, I believe you are the Son of God, that you died on the cross to rescue me from sin and death and to restore me to the Father. I choose now to turn from my sins, my self-centeredness, and every part of my life that does not please you. I choose you. I give myself to you. I receive your forgiveness and ask you to take your rightful place in my life as my Savior and Lord. Come reign in my heart, fill me with your love and your life, and help me to become a person who is truly loving—a person like you. Restore me, Jesus. Live in me. Love through me. Thank you, God. In Jesus' name, I pray. Amen.

I, _____, have repented of my sin, recognizing God loves me, and that Jesus died, was buried, and rose again. I have received the forgiveness of God and have asked Jesus to be my savior and am now born again this date: _____.

If you have prayed this prayer, I am excited for you and would love to know. Please send me an email to let me know you received Jesus as your personal savior.

LIVING LEGACY MINISTRIES
—INTERNATIONAL—

CONSIDER SUPPORTING

LIVING LEGACY MINISTRIES,

INTERNATIONAL

AND HELP US CREATE A

POSITIVE, LASTING CHANGE,

IN THE WORLD.

LIVING LEGACY MINISTRIES

Our ministry, Living Legacy Ministries, is creating a positive, lasting change in the world. One of the ways we do this is by drilling water wells and installing water filters in around the world.

Our inspiration. We used to pick up Mila, our granddaughter, from preschool every afternoon, and the first thing she would ask us is if we have a cup of iced cold water from Starbucks for her. She is hot, sweaty, and thirsty from playing on the playground. So, we always had a cup of water for her. We'd drive through Starbucks, order the water, drive to the window and they give it to us for free. It's just that simple.

<u>But not so simple for the over 840,000 children who die every year, from diarrhea, as a result of unsafe, contaminated drinking water, they are forced to drink.</u>

We decided we wanted to do something to help these children and provide clean water!

The wells we drill will be called Mila's Water Wells, developing a living, lasting legacy in her name!

Most water sources in developing countries are inadequate, and many of them are shared with animals from the local area. In fact, most of the sickness, disease, and death, is caused by fecal contamination from these very animals.

On average, women and children spend 200 million hours every day, collecting water that is already contaminated. Walking to fetch water is dangerous and treacherous. Many times, the walk can be an eight-mile round trip. And, when walking alone, women and young girls are vulnerable to sexual attacks.

When safe water becomes accessible, children can attend school, women have time to care for and earn money for their families, and sickness and disease are reduced.

**<u>The good news is you and I can make a difference!!!
There are three ways you can make a difference
and leave a living, lasting legacy</u>**

SPONSOR A WELL/LEAVE A LEGACY:

If you would like to sponsor a well for $4,500.00, a Legacy Nameplate with your name inscribed on it will be placed on the well, establishing a lasting family/business legacy!

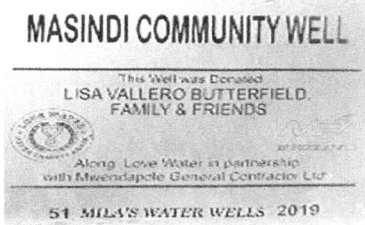

SPONSOR A WELL REPAIR/LEAVE A LEGACY:

We also have well-repair projects that are $1,500.00. We can repair a well that is in disrepair and restore clean water to a community. A Legacy Nameplate with your name inscribed on it will be placed on the well, establishing a lasting family/business legacy!

SPONSOR A WATER FILTER /LEAVE A LEGACY:

The cost to sponsor a water filter is only $100.00. Because of the low cost, many people and businesses sponsor several. Your name will be inscribed on each water filter.

You may send a check or donate at www.livinglegacyministries.com.

Thank you and God bless!

Pastor Mike & Estelle Martin

Living Legacy Ministries, International
2551 Galena Ave #1621
Simi Valley CA 93062
(805) 304-1155
Livinglegacyministries12@gmail.com
www.livinglegacyministries.com

Made in the USA
Middletown, DE
17 September 2024